D1563217

THE DAVENPORT CONSPIRACY REVISITED

THE
DAVENPORT CONSPIRACY
REVISITED

Marshall McKusick

IOWA STATE UNIVERSITY PRESS / AMES

Marshall McKusick is associate professor of anthropology, University of Iowa, Iowa City. He was State Archaeologist of Iowa from 1960 to 1975.

© 1991 Iowa State University Press, Ames, Iowa 50010
All rights reserved

Manufactured in the United States of America
∞ This book is printed on acid-free paper.

First edition, 1991

Library of Congress Cataloging-in-Publication Data

McKusick, Marshall Bassford
    The Davenport conspiracy revisited / Marshall McKusick.—1st ed.
      p. cm.
    Sequel to: The Davenport conspiracy.
    Includes bibliographical references and index.
    ISBN 0–8138–0344–6
    1. Mounds—Iowa. 2. Iowa—Antiquities. I. McKusick, Marshall Bassford. Davenport conspiracy. II. Title.
E78.I6M284   1991
977.7'01—dc20   90-40071

CONTENTS

FOREWORD

This new version of *The Davenport Conspiracy* lets us follow some fantastic archaeological machinations in eastern Iowa that began with the excavation of an interesting Indian mound in 1874 on the Cook Farm. However, this fascinating tale must first be put in its proper intellectual context.

American archaeology was nearly seventy-five years old when, in the 1850s, Samuel Haven sat down to write his comprehensive volume *Archaeology of the United States*—a somewhat inappropriate title since it was not a description of what was known but rather a review of archaeological history. The pursuit of America's past began in earnest in the 1780s after the Revolution, and by Haven's time sites had been mapped, artifacts had been described, and some sensible conclusions had been drawn. In Haven's view the problem of where the native Americans (he did not use that term) had come from was settled: from Asia via the "Behring" Strait.

The answer to the other major question, Who were the Mound Builders? was clear, at least to him: the makers of the earthen mounds and embankments, so well known in the Ohio Valley, were native Americans, not some fanciful transoceanic wayfarers. However, the chronology of these events was a mystery and, unfortunately, would remain so for many more decades.

The archaeology of the 1880s, which this volume treats, was quite different—as were the times themselves. The period of post–Civil War expansion of the economy and the nation itself, with the transcontinental railway system completed and America's industrial might growing swiftly, is known as the Gilded Age. But American archaeology, concentrated in the eastern states but soon to spread into the Southwest, was having a Golden Age.

More books, more sites, and more artifacts appeared as the prehistoric past became a fascination for well-to-do and well-educated amateurs. Throughout the Midwest they founded academies of science, in St. Louis, in Chicago, and even in Davenport, Iowa.

These institutions imitated the scientific societies of the East Coast that had flourished there for more than a century, such as the American Philosophical Society in Philadelphia and the American Antiquarian Society in Worcester, where Samuel Haven plied his trade.

It was a heady time for the young field of archaeology. There were no professionals yet—the first Ph.D.'s were decades into the future—so what constituted good archaeology depended on as yet unformalized standards. There were two prime questions: some still wondered, Who were the Mound Builders? but a new problem had sprung up, one concerning the age or dating of Early Man in America. (Remember that Paleolithic finds in Europe had just been made.) How should one judge the evidence?

Not that critical opinions or comments were absent from the annals of archaeology. Haven had known the literature with a breadth of coverage that still staggers the imagination of a modern-day, computer-assisted scholar. Haven also was not hesitant to identify what he thought was shoddy scholarship: he called these questionable volumes "vagaries," a rather quaint term. Today it's "pseudoarchaeology," or "Fantastic Archaeology" as I call it.

What Haven was concerned with was careless use of source material and problems of veracity. Those subjects remain major concerns today, as the present volume clearly indicates. Fraudulent materials (fakes) are lies: they lack the veracity that we have to depend on if we are to get our pictures of the past as correct as possible.

Now we all make mistakes, but we must have enough cross-checks to see that those errors are discovered before we go to press with a grand new interpretation of the past as known. Our conceptions of that past will change slowly as we gather new data, but we need to be able to believe that our foundation data, the information upon which all our later conclusions rest, are secure. The Davenport tablets are egregious fakes, and some said so right from the start, but that wasn't good enough to dispel the cloud of ill-advised belief surrounding them. It is a tale well told, now in an updated form by Marshall McKusick, and I shan't say more to spoil it for you.

Debunking is neither a pleasant nor an easy task—I share with Marshall that knowledge from hard experience. But it is a necessary one, and I don't think that he and I mind joining the ranks of the likes of Samuel Haven to press on with this now time-honored tradition. Marshall has done his homework; he has not taken second-hand sources when he could get to the originals. There are nuances of interpretation and personality that I do not share with the author, but the details of the case are carefully set forward; if you should choose to disagree, please come forward with new data in hand, not with Henshaw's bluster nor any special pleadings.

This is a case worth the time and effort that Marshall has given it; I only wish that many others would pick up the gauntlet that Haven threw down so long ago and dissect some more cases. I do know well the lengthy history of the Holly Oak gorget affair, also discussed herein; debunking isn't always neat and clean, but veracity will out, I feel sure. So now to Davenport and the peculiar finds of the Reverend Gass. Do they really solve the Mound Builder and the Early Man problems in one quick measure? Have a look.

STEPHEN WILLIAMS
Peabody Professor of American Archaeology
Harvard University

PREFACE

The Davenport Conspiracy Revisited is an archaeological mystery story—but fact rather than fiction—set in the 1880s, when the Smithsonian Institution staff confronted antiquarian delusions about the Mound Builders. The Smithsonian victory over the antiquarian speculations proved to be one of the major turning points in the foundation of professional archaeological research in the Americas; by the 1890s, the study of prehistory became the study of prehistoric Indians.

The Davenport Conspiracy, published in 1970, was well received by my professional colleagues and some years later went out of print. Meanwhile, there was a startling development when a marine biologist deluded the reading public in a series of books that resurrected the vintage Davenport frauds and used them as evidence that ancient Iowa had been explored thousands of years ago by Egyptians, Libyans, and Phoenicians. *The Davenport Conspiracy Revisited* is my reply to this contention.

Readers familiar with the original book will note that *The Davenport Conspiracy Revisited* was written for a wider audience; I have reduced the length of quoted documents, changed direct text citations to chapter notes, and incorporated the specimen appendix into the text in briefer form. In addition to these and other changes, the discussion concludes with the rebirth of antiquarian speculation and the rise of new mythologies about ancient times.

The 1970 preface acknowledged the now late Donald Herold, who located the original archival material and was director of the Davenport Museum in the 1960s, an institution now renamed the Putnam Museum. Others included Carol Hunt, museum registrar; Joseph Cartwright, a subsequent director; Frank Paluka, emeritus director of the University of Iowa Library Special Collections; J. N. Young; the late Irving Hurlbut of Muscatine, who provided one solution based upon discussions with Judge Bollinger; and Hertha Gass Erbe and Arthur Gass, both deceased, who provided background information about their father, the Reverend Jacob Gass, discoverer of the bogus artifacts in the 1870s that led others to create the Davenport Conspiracy. In the present book, I have benefited from discussions with David Meltzer, Southern Methodist University, as well as with my successors as State Archaeologist, Duane Anderson, Joseph Tiffany, and William Green. The Putnam Museum continues to be most helpful; I received assistance from Michael J. Smith, director, and Janice Hall, assistant director of curatorial services.

In recent years American archaeologists have taken greater interest in the historical development of their field of study. The contemporary development of pseudoscience has become a matter of concern. I refer professional colleagues to *Myth Makers: Epigraphic Illusion in America*, edited by James P. Whittall (Rowley, Maine: Early Sites Research Society, 1990). A more general discussion is found in *Frauds, Myths, and Mysteries: Science and Pseudoscience in Archaeology* by Kenneth L. Feder (Mountain View, Calif.: Mayfield Publishing, 1990). Another welcome addition is *Fantastic Archaeology: The Wild Side of American Archaeology*, forthcoming from the University of Pennsylvania Press. I am pleased that its author, Prof. Stephen Williams, has written the foreword to *The Davenport Conspiracy Revisited.*

Finally, I acknowledge the sincere efforts of Marshall Payne of Pratt College, San Diego, whose correspondence with me is filed with other documents on the case in Special Collections, University of Iowa Library. Payne attempted to demonstrate the likelihood that one of the old slate shingles is written in ancient Libyan and thus represents a genuine record of ancient voyagers to the Cook Farm mounds. My own study forces me to reject this claim without equivocation.

THE DAVENPORT CONSPIRACY REVISITED

1

An Iowa Solution to the Mound Builder Mystery

When Christopher Columbus explored the west Atlantic islands, he named the newfound sea the Caribbean after the fierce Carib tribesmen. Columbus believed he had found the Atlantic sealane to India and was navigating in that subcontinent's island approaches, so he named the islands the *Indies* and their inhabitants *Indians*. These names, despite the immensity of the geographical error, continue in use to the present time. The natives, of course, were not Indians of India—and so the question arose as to the relationship of the natives to the rest of humanity. According to the Bible, all humankind descended from Adam and Eve, until the Great Flood destroyed the human race with the sole exception of Noah and his descendants. Judeo-Christian theology taught that all Old World nations were Noachites, tracing their origins back to Noah's ark. But were the New World natives also descended from Noah?

In the first decades of Spanish conquest in the 1500s, theological interpretation took on crucial importance in determining native civil rights. If native Americans were Noachites, descended from Adam and Eve through Noah, all would be well for them. However, if no biblical interpretation fitted the case, the natives were in a bad way, totally unrelated to the rest of humanity. In this situation, the natives would be pre-Adamites, and theologians could not explain their existence. The issue had grave implications—pre-Adamites might look human but they were inhuman. The resolution of bibli-

cal theology on the Indian question would determine European rela-
tions with the rest of humanity. Without linkage with the rest of humanity,
the natives lacked human rights and, moreover, could never hope to
acquire them.

Spanish plantation owners could use Christian theology to justify perpetual native slavery. However, the Spanish priests were ac-
tively converting the natives to Christianity, conversions that were
meaningless if native Americans lacked human status. An adminis-
trative rule was needed that gave theological recognition of Noachite status to the American Indians. The matter was soon resolved,
and at the highest theological level: in 1537 the papal bull by Pope
Paul III proclaimed the human status of the American Indians and
encouraged the spread of Christianity among them.[1] Paradoxically,
theology sanctioned the importation of black African slaves. The
natives, however, became the equivalent of serfs, a higher status
that allowed more upward social mobility to their descendants under Spanish rule.

Pope Paul III justified native civil rights in 1537 by attributing
native descent from the Ten Lost Tribes of Israel, the origin myth
that continues to have some viability today among those who are
unaware of, or not convinced by, archaeological facts. The Ten Lost
Tribes myth represents one of the earliest of numerous European
speculations about native origins.

A more secular, nonbiblical explanation about the natives also
appears early in European thought, the theme of which is Lost
Atlantis. The Greek philosopher Plato either invented or retold the
myth of Lost Atlantis, an island or continent from which an ad-
vanced civilization had launched an invasion into the Mediterranean lands. This tale, retold in subsequent classical literature, reappeared in the European Renaissance. By the 1530s, and thereafter
up until the present time, the imaginary Atlantis became the
oceanic home of a race who subsequently settled the Americas.
During the next centuries, rival theories rose and waned in popular-
ity, sharing the stage with mysterious Atlantis and the Ten Lost
Tribes. Some attempted to trace native descent from ancient Scandinavia, others to the Scythians of Central Asia, while other entries
to the game included Celts, Egyptians, Phoenicians, Greeks, Ko-
reans, Chinese, and Pacific Islanders. The guess that the Americas
had been peopled either by land or sea from eastern Asia was less
exotic and consequently less popular as an explanation. Nevertheless, it is interesting to note that the Asiatic route to America was
first proposed in 1590 and favored the suggestion of a migration by

land.[2] This, of course, is the anthropological-archaeological explanation for the arrival of the Paleo-Indians across Beringia, the ancient land bridge between present day Siberia and Alaska.

To understand the beginnings of archaeological exploration in the United States during the nineteenth century, it must be emphasized that the key issue lay in the origin of the American Indians, and more specifically in the relationship between prehistoric earthworks and the Indians. For nearly a century, the major question in North American archaeology was the identification of the Mound Builders.[3]

Major John Wesley Powell, a one-armed Civil War veteran—and at various times a geologist, explorer, and naturalist—was the first director of the Bureau of American Ethnology, a department of the Smithsonian Institution. Among his lasting contributions was organizing research to conclusively demonstrate that prehistoric Indians built the North American earthworks. He and his colleagues rejected the fanciful theories about lost Israelites or civilized European invaders settling North America in ancient times.

Reviewing the problem of Mound Builders in an 1894 publication, Major Powell noted that many prominent Americans were intrigued with the origins of the still-mysterious earthworks. Benjamin Franklin, for instance, was inclined to attribute mound building to de Soto and other Spanish explorers. Noah Webster originally agreed with Franklin but later changed his mind when reports came in that huge artificial earthworks were common rather than rare. This fact led Webster to conclude that Indians built the mounds, and others agreed, among them Thomas Jefferson. In addition, at least two other presidents had been interested in the mound problem, George Washington and Benjamin Harrison.

Major Powell considered Dr. Benjamin S. Barton to be the first to advance the theory of "lost races" in his book *New Views on the Origin of the Tribes of America*, published in 1798. Barton reasoned that the mounds were not built by either the living Indians or their predecessors but by a people with a higher "cultivation" who had established law and order with a well-disciplined police.[4]

During the nineteenth century, many antiquarians thought themselves authorities on the subject of Mound Builders, and these writers had little or no knowledge beyond speculations. Those who more seriously examined the evidence came to quite different opinions. Some concluded that the mounds and earthworks were built by the ancestors of the historic tribes visited by European explorers, while others thought that the mounds were left by Pueblo Indians,

Toltecs, Aztecs, or even more distant peoples, perhaps from the civilizations of Europe or Asia. In the midst of this controversy, Ephraim Squire and Edwin Hamilton Davis wrote a landmark study, *Ancient Monuments in the Mississippi Valley*, published in 1848 as the first monograph in the famous Contributions to Knowledge series issued by the Smithsonian Institution. The study carried the weight of respected authority. Squire and Davis held that there were two distinct races, Mound Builder and Indian, a conclusion that was used for years by armchair antiquarians to justify speculations about the origin of the mysterious Mound Builders.

A closer reading of the report shows that Squire and Davis did not intend to have their report open the door to such speculative interpretations. They clearly regarded the Mound Builders to be native Americans, although different from the tribes inhabiting the same regions at the time of European discovery. They concluded, "We may venture to suggest that the facts thus far collected point to a connection more or less intimate between the race of the mounds and the semicivilized nations which formerly had their seats among the Sierras of Mexico, and upon the plains of Central America and Peru."[5] This connection was too broadly stated, for it was nonsense to relate mound building to the Central Americans and Peruvians. It was oversimplified and not confirmed by modern research. Yet there was a kernel of truth to their observations about Mexican influence.

A number of burial mounds explored during the nineteenth century would now be assigned to two cultural climaxes of indigenous religion, Adena and Hopewell, named after type sites in Ohio. A vast intertribal trade network had developed to support Hopewell burial rituals during a period from about 300 B.C. to A.D. 300, and this religious activity occurred over a vast region of eastern North America. The closer examination of Hopewell religious practices shows that there were regional subtraditions that varied from one area to the next. For example, there were differences in tomb construction and ritual. One of the commonalities of Hopewell was the practice of placing grave goods with some of the more prominent deceased. When such offerings were made, they sometimes included materials from far distant sources, such as Gulf Coast marine shells, Appalachian mica, Ohio pipestone, Minnesota catlinite pipestone, Great Lakes copper, brown chalcedony from western North Dakota, and Wyoming obsidian. In addition, there was a special mortuary pottery placed with some of the dead that was decorated with large raptorial birds and other motifs, combined with stamped and impressed decoration.[6] Whether or not cultural inspiration from Mexican centers of civilization stimulated the growth of Hopewell religion is a matter that has been debated in the more recent technical reports on archaeological sites. Although a case can be made for the Mexican origin of some cultural traits found in Hopewell sites, majority archaeological opinion holds that the Hopewell manifestation was an indigenous culture. It is enough here to emphasize that in the nineteenth century, the Hopewell mounds were not recognized as a native, prehistoric burial ceremonialism. The mounds were assigned to the race of Mound Builders.

From the perspective of modern archaeological findings, there is a second major mound tradition, the Mississippian. The Mississippian tradition spread through the upper Midwest long after the Hopewell manifestation became dormant. Dates are variously given, but in its characteristic form Mississippian culture began to be widespread after A.D. 900 and in some areas continued up to the time of the European explorations.[7] This Mississippian tradition was typified by the presence of ceremonial centers with multiple temple-mound earthworks and plazas closely resembling some found in Mexico. A much greater reliance was placed upon agriculture than in earlier times, and Mississippian peoples grew Mexican-derived varieties of maize, beans, and squash. Despite the obvious Mexican cultural imports of agricultural technology and temple-mound construction, however, archaeologists today view the Mississippian tradition as a series of individually variable, regional subtraditions, and consider much of Mississippian culture as indigenous to the areas where it appeared.[8]

The nineteenth-century mound diggers were unable to properly sort out the evidence from the excavations. The early research failed to distinguish between Hopewell, Mississippian, and other manifestations. All of the mounds and earthworks were lumped together as remains left by the ancient race of Mound Builders. The Mexican influences remarked upon by Squire and Davis were Mississippian and not characteristic of the earlier Hopewell burial-mound tradition. Even those Mexican influences were misunderstood. The Mississippian sites were not the result of Aztec colonizations or similar migrations from as far away as Peru. The misconceptions of Squire and Davis unfortunately led to even greater errors because they strengthened the notion that there had been a separate race of Mound Builders distinct from the later abori-

ginal tribes. The myth of the Mound Builders was then elaborated
by others who always cited Squire and Davis as a major source. A
few men continued to argue that indigenous prehistoric Indians had
built the mounds, and one of the spokesmen for this position was
Samuel Haven in his report of 1855.[9] Unfortunately, the Mound
Builder myth was a more attractive and dramatic theory. It was also
more in keeping with the nineteenth-century stereotype of "redskins" who were too indifferent, lazy, and disorganized to have built
the imposing earthworks. One key phrase, "white Indians," sum-
marizes the racism that led antiquarians to look far afield for some
superior race that had held sway in North America until its power
was shattered by local "savages" (figure 1.1).[10] If white Indians had
built the mounds, then it seemed possible to some writers that ancient European white men had somehow arrived long before Columbus and had brought civilization with them from across the ocean.

If civilized Mound Builders had come from across the Atlantic, there should be monumental inscriptions, the written word, an ancient Mediterranean or European language preserved on stone. Could such records of the past be found? Thousands of treasure seekers and amateur antiquarians ransacked the North American burial mounds, tearing them apart and destroying them in the search for the stone tablets that some predicted would give a written account of the last days of the Mound Builders before they were overrun by untamed hordes of newcomers to America—none other

1.1. Ancient American "battlemound." While women and children anxiously await the outcome on top of the mound, the civilized Mound Builders on the lower platforms fight off hordes of "savage redskins." This engraving typifies the myth of the Mound Builders. (Pidgeon 1852)

than the familiar North American Indians. This incredible tale of antiquity not only led to mound plundering but encouraged a genre of science fiction, eagerly read by part of the public, which told of the prehistoric life-and-death struggles between white civilization and red savagery.[11]

The results of roughshod mound explorations astonished some skeptics of the Mound Builder tales, because a few examples of ancient writing were found on stone tablets and outcrops. Each case generated controversy between supporters and doubters. Some examples were later to be identified as simple rock drawings made by Indians, drawings termed pictographs and petroglyphs. The famous Dighton Rock near Fall River, Massachusetts, was first seen by early colonists, and its "writing" has puzzled antiquarians since the late 1700s. Over the years its "message" has variously been interpreted as Phoenician, Norse runic, early Portuguese, or one of many other languages. Dighton Rock actually had some prehistoric Algonkian-type petroglyph designs overlaid by more modern graffiti, such as the alleged Old Norse inscription that reads in English, "This way to the spring."[12]

Other examples of writing on stone found by the antiquarians were not in any known script but were simply lines cut into stone from erosion, frost spalling, or glacial scratches. A few examples were neither natural markings nor aboriginal petroglyphs, and these generated the most heated controversies. One such example, alleged to be from a mound in Ohio, was a stone tablet written in modern Hebrew that lacked weathering or other signs of antiquity. Found in the early post–Civil War period during the height of speculation about white Indians, this Holy Stone of Warwick, as it was named, came to be widely accepted as proof that the lost race of Mound Builders had been Noachite Israelites.[13]

Mound explorers of Anglo-Saxon origin who might be equally prejudiced against Indians, white Indians, and Israelites, could point to a different discovery for the origin of the lost Mound Builders. The ethnic hopes of this group lay in the mysterious Grave Creek tablet, a very small, ornament-sized inscription that reportedly had been found in the very bowels of a sixty-foot high burial mound on the bank of the Ohio River, in what became the state of West Virginia. This remarkable fraud from the 1830s, the Grave Creek tablet, had a mixture of alphabetic letters of reputed Germanic, Old Irish, or other Indo-European origin. Long after the numerous quarrels about the proper decipherment of the Grave Creek tablet had reached a stalemate, it was discovered that the tablet had been carved and put into the Grave Creek Museum to encourage visitors to pay admission and see Mound Builder relics.[14]

In the late 1870s, in the midst of the great antiquarian Mound Builder debate, two slate tablets were found in a burial mound on the Cook Farm near Davenport, Iowa. One of the tablets was clearly inscribed with a European or Mediterranean type of zodiac, complete with circles and the proper signs. The zodiac was of obvious Old World derivation and unlike any known astronomical monuments of aboriginal origin. The second slate tablet was of even greater interest, for it contained shallow, partly scrawled letters in script, hastily drawn, in some form of alphabet variously identified by eager antiquarians as Hittite, Phoenician, or some other written language of Near Eastern or Mediterranean origin. One author wrote that he could identify the writing as coming from China or Korea. The antiquarian decipherments were not in agreement, but on one point there was near unanimity. If the slate tablet discovery was genuine and not a modern forgery, and if it dated from prehistoric times, then it could be confirmed that the Mound Builder question was finally resolved. The Mound Builders had indeed migrated to ancient America from some Mediterranean land. The prompt publication of excellent photographs of the slate tablets heightened public and scholarly interest in the unique discovery.[15]

What did these Mound Builders look like and how were they dressed? These questions were promptly answered by another discovery from a different Cook Farm mound. Inside that mound was a crude altar built of limestone blocks, and within the altar, in a specially constructed cavity, there was a large limestone tablet inscribed with the smiling face of a presumed Mound Builder. The carving was part of the complete figure of a Mound Builder, painted red like an Indian and dressed in nothing at all (see figure 4.2).[16]

How old were the Mound Builders? At the time of the discovery in Davenport, mammoth and mastodon had been found with Paleolithic Stone-Age tools in Europe. There were also discoveries of the extinct mammoth and mastodon in North America. The archaeological evidence of stone tools associated with these North American elephants was controversial. Some, if not most, antiquarians were convinced that firmer evidence would be found absolutely proving that the earliest populations of prehistoric North America had come to the continent at a time prior to the elephant extinctions. This great controversy was now resolved at the archaeologi-

cal diggings in Iowa. From Louisa County, south of Davenport, a
farmer found a small effigy pipe carved from limestone. The carving
clearly depicted *either a mammoth or a mastodon*—it was impossible to identify the elephant more closely because the effigy lacked
tusks. The excitement heightened when another mound yielded up
a second example of a tobacco pipe carved in the form of a shaggy,
tuskless, Pleistocene elephant.[17]

The remarkable stone tablets and elephant-shaped pipes were
found under the sponsorship of a local amateur scientific club, the
Davenport Academy of Natural Sciences (figure 1.2). This research

1.2.   *The Davenport Academy at the time of the conspiracy. Completed in 1878, this building on Brady Street was finally demol-
ished in the late 1960s when a large modern museum was built in
a new location. (Putnam Museum)*

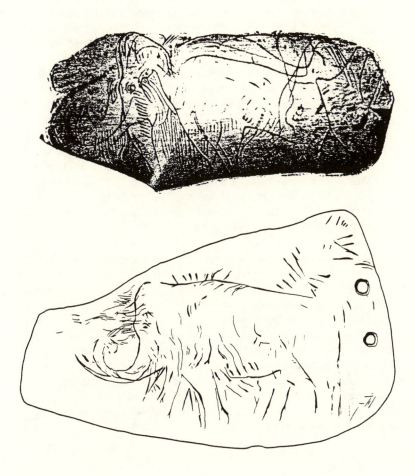

1.3. Discovered in 1865, the Magdalenian engraving (upper) became known to American readers through the classic Prehistoric
Times by Sir John Lubbock, in his second edition of 1869. The
American Holly Oak mammoth (lower) is an 1889 forgery based
upon Lubbock's imperfect reproduction of French publications.
(Meltzer and Sturtevant 1983:330–31; courtesy of the authors and
 the Museum of Anthropology, University of Michigan, Ann Arbor)

brought the Academy into national prominence; the findings were widely discussed in leading scholarly journals in the United States, and these discussions were republished abroad, in England's *Nature* and in *Zeitschrift für Ethnologie*, the most prestigious anthropological journal in Germany.[18] The Davenport Academy discoveries, *if accepted as genuine*, resolved the Mound Builder contentions of the day.

The Davenport Pleistocene elephant effigies closely copied the mammoth drawn on a tusk found at the Magdalenian type site of the Upper Paleolithic in France. This famous French artifact, discovered in 1865, was reproduced in contemporary textbooks in English (figure 1.3). The Davenport effigies, appearing in 1878 and 1880, were soon followed by other successful frauds modeled on the Magdalenian mammoth drawing. The Lenape Stone from the Delaware Valley first made its appearance in print in 1885, and the Holly Oak site in Delaware provided another example in 1889, a shell pendant engraved with the "French" mammoth. Both were frauds but both generated controversy.[19]

Meanwhile, the earlier Davenport discoveries convinced many antiquarians that a mysterious civilized race had first settled in the upper Mississippi Valley when mammoth lived on the premises. Rival decipherments of the tablets led to opinions that the Mound Builders immigrated into North America from Europe, the Near East, or even Korea. Davenport diggings seemingly confirmed Pope Paul's 1537 decision about the Noachite ancestry of the Indians. Science fiction of the 1840s appeared to be scientific fact in the 1880s, and there was something for everyone. The Davenport artifacts fulfilled prophecy, verified papal dictum, confirmed fiction about white Indians, and moreover dumbfounded the "relic sharps" at the Smithsonian Institution[20]—a perfect ending it seemed, and all so very scientific.

2

DISCOVERY OF THE SLATE TABLETS

The director of archaeology at the Smithsonian Bureau of Ethnology during the 1880s and 1890s was Cyrus Thomas. In his extensive monograph of 1894 on mound explorations, he wrote that a majority of antiquarians believed that the mounds had been built by a comparatively civilized people. The question had been widely discussed that these people had lived at the time of the Pleistocene elephants. Another unsettled question was the purpose of stone altars found in the Ohio mounds. Cyrus Thomas then continued by discussing the Davenport affair with mocking language:

> Suddenly the archaeological world is surprised at finding itself in possession of proof on all these points. A tablet is taken from a mound under the very shadow of one of our leading scientific academies on which is an inscription of sufficient length to silence all doubt as to its being alphabetic, and immediately under it is the altar with the smoking sacrifice or burning body on it. Nay, more, on the reverse is the figure of the elephant. Nor is this all. In the same mound is another tablet with markings for the zodiacal signs, a calendar in fact. But good fortune, not satisfied with this generosity, throws into the hands of the same individual two elephant pipes, so distinct that there can be no doubt as to the animal intended. To clinch this evidence and show that it relates to the true mound builders, the fairy goddess leads the same hands to a mound which contains a tablet bearing figures of the veritable mound builders' pipes and copper axe, some of

the letters on the other tablet and the sun symbol. Thanks to the energy of one person the evidence on all these questions is furnished, which, if accepted as credible, must forever settle them.[1]

The question hung upon the phrase *if accepted as credible.* The Davenport discoveries represented one of the most bitterly contested interpretations in American archaeology. Cyrus Thomas, the leading professional archaeologist in America, poured oil on fire by his gratuitous description of a *fairy goddess* holding hands with the unnamed mound explorer, Reverend Jacob Gass. In a similar vein, another Bureau of Ethnology staff member, Henry Henshaw, published a comment about the *remarkable divining rod* that Reverend Gass might have used, a charge without any substantiation.[2] Equally exuberant statements by Cyrus Thomas appeared in correspondence under official letterhead, letters that sometimes circulated beyond the individuals to whom they were addressed. Both the *fairy goddess* and *divining rod* comments appeared in the Smithsonian *Bureau of Ethnology Reports,* an official publication that antiquarian defenders considered to represent a government-sponsored attack upon a helpless private citizen. The lawyer leading the defense of Reverend Gass and his discoveries, Charles Putnam, was equally quick to defame the Smithsonian in rebuttal. The controversy became personal.

Who was the discoverer of the unique Davenport artifacts? The publications of the day provide very little background. In the course of my investigation, I talked with his daughter, the late Hertha Gass Erbe of Postville, Iowa.[3] The Reverend Jacob Gass was born in 1842 in Oltingen, Switzerland, and studied theology in Basel (figure 2.1). In 1868, while still a young man, he emigrated from Switzerland to the United States, continuing his theological training at Wartburg Seminary, then located in Strawberry Point, Iowa. Ordained in 1871, he began his career at the First Lutheran Church in Davenport, at that time a bustling community of about thirty thousand. This background would be irrelevant, except that Davenport had a very large German-speaking population. Reverend Gass preached and taught in German and was not yet fluent in English. His written archaeological reports were brief, seldom more than a few sentences long, and translated by others into English at the Davenport Academy of Natural Sciences.[4] He was, in short, a prodigious digger, but he was not an archaeologist even by the loose standards of his day.

2.1.   Rev. Jacob Gass (1842–1924). (Photograph courtesy of his daughter, the late Hertha Gass Erbe)

There were no important works on North American archaeology published in German, and it appears that what information he had about prehistoric America was obtained at second hand from English-speaking colleagues at the Davenport Academy. Of equal importance to understanding the controversy was the fact that the Academy was the stronghold of easterners—New York and New England Yankees—and they were generally contemptuous of the German immigrants who had moved into Davenport in great numbers. When Reverend Gass appeared at the Academy, he encountered a great deal of prejudice. Hot tempered and prone to making enemies, Reverend Gass deliberately insulted some of the members by telling them that they did not work hard enough when digging mounds. He apparently told them in his thick German accent that he was able to find wonderful mound treasures, while they were too lazy to find anything of interest. This led to the retort, preserved by local tradition, that Gass made the artifacts he claimed to dig out of the mounds and that the clergyman was a "windjammer and liar."[5]

Under these circumstances, it is surprising that Reverend Gass was elected to Academy membership in 1876 and became a trustee several years later. He was the only German-speaking immigrant among the Yankees for some years, until his brother-in-law, Reverend Adolph Blumer, was admitted. The election of Reverend Gass occurred in the following way.

After arriving in Davenport as a Lutheran clergyman in 1871 or 1872, Reverend Gass became curious about the prehistoric burial mounds. He unquestionably knew about the Swiss Lake Dwellers in his homeland, most likely from visits to sites near his home and Basel, where he later studied. During the middle of the nineteenth century, some of the lakes in Switzerland, Germany, and France had receded, and archaeologists recognized wooden pilings that supported small houses in use during the Neolithic and Bronze ages. These finds in his homeland may have spurred him to excavate mound sites in his new country.[6] In 1874 he excavated several mounds on the Cook Farm on a point of land overlooking the Mississippi River, a site then located on the outskirts of Davenport but today located near the center of town and covered by a factory.[7] He was assisted by his brother-in-law (a man named Borgelt, who was also a Lutheran clergyman) and two young men identified only as theological students. These mound explorations uncovered a remarkable series of artifacts.

Reports of the 1874 Cook Farm discoveries by Reverend Gass and his colleagues first appeared in Davenport German-language newspapers.[8] But word of the excavations quickly reached the English-speaking community, and a prominent member of the Davenport Academy became most interested. His name was Dr. Robert Farquharson, and he visited the excavation in its final stages and introduced himself to the excavators. Reverend Gass had no interest in publishing a scientific report, and Dr. Farquharson persuaded the clergyman to turn over the materials to him so that he could write a description of the excavations and the specimens. This resulted in a lengthy publication in the prestigious *Proceedings of the American Association for the Advancement of Science* in 1875, in which much of the discussion centered upon prehistoric copper axes and the preserved examples of textiles adhering to them.[9] Dr. Farquharson insisted that Reverend Gass be permitted to join the Academy, and he arranged for several prominent sponsors to back the nomination. There was some opposition because of the insults the clergyman had directed at other mound explorers, and Reverend Gass did not receive election to membership until 1876, two years following his Cook Farm mound discoveries. The artifacts from the excavation were either sold or donated to the Academy and are still in the Putnam Museum. After election to membership, Jacob Gass worked for the Academy from 1877 to 1882, on both a volunteer and a paid basis. He also worked on his own account, trading and selling relics to other collectors as late as 1881.[10]

The description of the 1874 Cook Farm excavations written by Dr. Farquharson was based partly upon the doctor's own limited observations at the site and also upon the newspaper accounts, which were incomplete and sketchy.[11] The drawings of the specimens were prepared by the owner of a local Davenport business college, William Pratt, and they were out of proportion and somewhat crude. In coming years, Pratt was to abandon his business college in order to become the first full-time, paid curator of the Academy (figure 2.2). When the clergyman's later discoveries became controversial, Pratt was the curator and became the right-

2.2.   *William H. Pratt (1822–1892). One of the three original founders of the Academy, he served his term as president in 1880 and shortly after became the Academy's first full-time, paid curator. (Putnam Museum)*

hand man of the lawyer, Charles Putnam, in the defense of the specimens and the cover-up that became the Davenport conspiracy.[12]

Because of the local interest in the Cook Farm discoveries of
1874, Dr. Farquharson's publication in the *Proceedings of the
American Association for the Advancement of Science* of 1875 was
reprinted in the first volume of *Proceedings of the Davenport Academy of Natural Sciences,* published the next year.[13] Despite the novelty and uniqueness of the discoveries, the publication was amateurish and inadequate by the standards of the time, and moreover
contained errors and inconsistencies. Dr. Farquharson had to rely
upon accounts at second hand, a problem that would continue
when describing the further work of Reverend Gass, who found that
note writing interfered with the speed of his excavations.

Throughout the 1874 excavations and during the time Dr.
Farquharson prepared his report, Jacob Gass modestly declined to
interpret his discoveries. He was content to leave such matters to
those who felt themselves better qualified. He considered his forte to
be mound exploration, the recovery of artifacts. He was young,
trim, strong, and energetic, and although not a large or heavily
muscled man, he very much enjoyed the outdoor activity that
mound exploring gave him—in later years, when problems forced
him out of the ministry, he was well satisfied with his outdoor life as
a farmer in Postville, Iowa, where he raised his family. He did not
enjoy writing excavation reports and never prepared a contemporary account of his 1874 excavations, although he later wrote a
few comments about them.[14] This same pattern—a lack of written
documentation about his work—persisted through all of his subsequent excavations carried out under Academy sponsorship. Three
years later, in 1877, when he returned to the Cook Farm and found
the inscribed slate tablets that lay at the heart of the Davenport
conspiracy, Reverend Gass had to be persuaded to write up an account of the discovery (an account that later proved to be incomplete). A year later, when the inscribed limestone tablet was found,
it was his associate, Charles Harrison, who prepared the report.[15] In
this way, Reverend Gass attempted to remain in the background,
unobtrusively providing unique relics for others to describe and interpret.

His behavior led those who considered his artifacts to be false to
regard the clergyman as masterminding a plot to promote theories
about lost races of Mound Builders. But there seems to be a simpler
explanation. Reverend Gass did not speak English fluently and
wrote only in German, his letters and reports having to be trans-

lated prior to publication. He was eloquent in German and also wrote poetry, but his temperament was not well suited to the preparation of detailed, descriptive reports. In short, the discoverer of the unique relics of Mound Builders was energetic and vain; furthermore, he considered himself a poet and did not like the drudgery of writing reports. There is no evidence that he was particularly interested in the Mound Builder speculations or even well informed about them. He was a digger who enjoyed the out-of-doors; a clergyman who saw no ethical conflict in selling a fraud to a fellow relic hunter; a man who was not a scientist, not even an amateur one.

The 1874 excavation at Cook Farm centered on Mound 3, so numbered in a map later prepared by the curator, William Pratt (figure 2.3). It was the largest of the mound group, measuring fifty-five feet across and seven feet high. Most of the artifacts were found in the southern half of the mound; the remaining half was left unexcavated until 1877. Reverend Gass and his companions apparently shoveled right through two historic-period Indian graves (identified as such by the presence of European trade beads and jewelry). These two burials were not examined. Beneath them, the explorers found older skeletons and numerous artifacts, but the excavation continued at a fast pace, no plan of the skeletons being prepared, not even an unquestioned count of the individual interments present. Some of the burials were extended in horizontal positions, and other skeletons were flexed in what the explorers reported to be sitting positions. The bones apparently lay in normal anatomical positions rather than being disturbed and scattered throughout the mound. Burial rituals were indicated by the presence of stone groupings termed "altars," limestone slabs laid over or around the burial areas, as well as layers of shell and ash.[16]

The artifacts included mortuary pottery now recognized as Havana Hopewell ceramics and superb examples of flintwork. There were other examples of bone and shell artifacts and two effigy platform pipes, one of them in the form of an animal variously identified as a groundhog, dog, or wolf. Various awl-like tools of copper were found, as well as five copper axes that had a coarse encrustation over them. At least one of these axes was polished up, and the others were about to undergo a similar fate when Dr. Farquharson intervened by observing that this encrustation required closer attention. He identified the presence of cloth fabric preserved by its contact with the copper, the axes originally having a bag or wrapping to protect them at the time of burial. The textile identification gave Dr. Farquharson's report some importance. The southern half

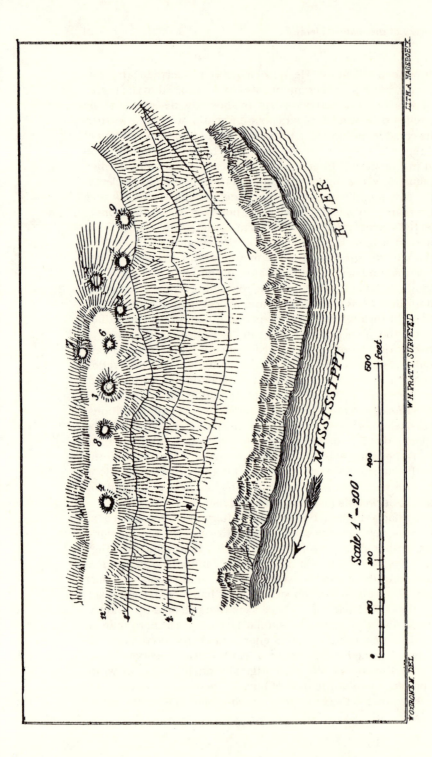

2.3. *Cook Farm mounds, Davenport. This survey by the Academy curator, W. H. Pratt, documented the 1874 excavations by Rev. Jacob Gass and is the earliest published instrument survey of an archaeological site in Iowa. (Farquharson 1876, pl. 1)*

of Mound 3 was only part of the 1874 excavations at the Cook Farm site. Other mounds provided similar finds and included additional examples of both effigy and plain platform pipes, Havana Hopewell pottery, and copper and stone artifacts.[17]

In view of the later debacle that developed over fraudulent artifacts, it is important to emphasize here that the specimens obtained by Reverend Gass in 1874 were genuine. I have personally examined the artifacts, and they represent a collection of Hopewell burial objects of great rarity. A number of pipes were made of green-gray pipestone typical of Hopewellian pipes in Ohio. Dr. Henry Shetrone, director of the Ohio Museum in the 1920s and 1930s, studied the collection and considered the material to be traded into Iowa from Ohio.[18] Some of these platform pipes were beautifully shaped to resemble animals—a bird, a frog, and a doglike effigy.[19] The plain platform pipes were perfectly proportioned and finished.

In addition to the Ohio pipestone, there were other trade goods—including obsidian, presumably from Wyoming quarries, and marine shell from the Gulf Coast. The copper came from aboriginal mines or perhaps from outcrops situated around the Lake Superior basin. Radiocarbon chronology suggests that this trade in Hopewell grave goods occurred from approximately 300 B.C. to A.D. 300. The kinds of discoveries made by Reverend Gass have rarely been found in Iowa. Hopewellian ceramics appear in mounds along the Mississippi River bluffs and sporadically inland along the Des Moines River, but platform pipes seldom occur. A few were found in mounds along the Iowa River in northeast Iowa, and a single example was reported from Webster County in central Iowa.[20] All other examples known to me come from a restricted area of southeast Iowa, from large mounds on the Mississippi bluffs between Davenport and Burlington some fifty miles downstream. There has been a great deal of mound excavation by both amateurs and professionals in the century since Reverend Gass opened the Cook Farm mounds, and no one has found anything that equals the quantity and quality of the cult objects he discovered. He was incredibly fortunate in choosing a site for his first excavations, but his Cook Farm finds were nevertheless genuine.

In January 1877, only months after his election to Academy membership, Reverend Gass returned to his excavations at the Cook Farm. An Iowa winter was an odd time for archaeological investigations, and even a century ago it required a published explanation when the finds became controversial. As has been mentioned, the clergyman's abrasive remarks made many enemies; some were inside the Academy, and others lived in the Davenport area. It appears that the lease on the Cook Farm was due to expire and the new tenant had sworn to friends that he would never allow Reverend Gass on the property. Some of the Academy members repeated this threat to the clergyman; it was a dig-now-or-never situation, and they urged him to excavate before it was too late. There was only one obvious place to dig, the northern half of Mound 3, left over because of its size when the southern half was cleared in 1874. Rather than allow any part of the mound to remain for other relic hunters in the Academy, Gass decided to finish the job himself, regardless of difficulties. The published statement on the excavation gave the change of tenant as the reason for the wintry mound excursion.[21] More to the point, Academy Yankees urged Gass to dig and seemingly emphasized the most propitious spot to try his luck, but they did not come out to watch the Germans have a go at relic hunting.

It was an incredible time to carry out fieldwork, but Reverend Gass arrived with seven German friends, and they smashed through two-and-one-half feet of the frozen ground and poked a hole into the remnant of the mound. They first encountered another historic Indian burial *with the bones scattered and disturbed,* and they picked up some glass beads and part of a brass ring, which were European trade goods. Digging deeper, they next found two layers of shells, which they threw out of the hole, and uncovered a burial pit *with loose black soil.* It contained some human bone fragments and bits of slate. The skeletons, like those in the historic burial, were in disorder. This was unlike the complete skeletons excavated from the southern half of Mound 3 in 1874. Gass later wrote a brief report that was published in English translation by the Academy. He wrote of finding the disturbed burials and the loose soil:

> These circumstances arrested particular attention, and caused me to proceed with more caution, until soon after—about five o'clock in the afternoon—we discovered the two inscribed tablets of coal slate. . . . The smaller one is engraved on one side only, and the larger on both sides. The larger one was lying with that side upward which was somewhat injured by a stroke with the spade. . . . Both were closely encircled by a row of limestones. They were covered on both sides with clay, on removal of which the markings were for the first time discovered. . . . It should also be remarked that I did not leave the mound after penetrating through the frost until the tablets were discovered and taken from their resting place with my own hands.[22]

The entire excavation, including breaking up the frozen ground over the northern burial pit of Mound 3, was accomplished in a single winter's day. The tablets were found at 5 P.M. in approaching darkness. We can picture the clergyman and his friends, all eight of them, groping about in a black, craterlike hole, shoveling and banging rocks with their spades. The excavation was a travesty of archaeological techniques even a century ago, and the slate tablets demonstrate this. The inscribed surface of the Calendar stone is scarred with at least one shovel cut, and the margins are battered (figure 2.4). The other slate tablet broke along an interior cleavage

2.4. The Calendar stone, excavated from Mound 3 in 1877. (Putnam Museum specimen AR-15341)

plane after a solid hit, so that the front and back inscribed surfaces were separated (figures 2.5 and 2.6). The uppermost side, with the inscribed Cremation Scene, was broken in half once more by a spade blow. Both sides were additionally scarred, and the tablet margins are completely missing on one side and gouged off on parts of the other three edges.[23] There is mention of the bits of slate lying about, and there was no effort made in picking them up to piece together a restoration of the larger slate tablet. It is not unlikely that

2.5. *The Cremation Scene tablet, the obverse side of a single piece of slate split during the hasty digging by Rev. Gass and his companions. (Putnam Museum specimen AR-15338)*

some of the slate fragments might have been a third tablet destroyed during the chase. An Academy representative, William Pratt, visited the abandoned diggings the day after and in the back dirt found a strange concretion resembling an animal with glued-on quartz crystals to represent eyes (see figure 13.8).[24] This specimen was to foreshadow the discovery of an inscribed limestone tablet in January 1878, a year later.

2.6.   *The Hunting Scene tablet, the reverse side of the piece of slate bearing the Cremation Scene. (Putnam Museum specimen AR-15339)*

This battering of specimens despite protection by a clay covering serves as evidence that the clergyman had no prior knowledge of the contents of the disturbed burial pit. If he had any intimations of the discovery, the work would have progressed more cautiously in the vicinity of the remarkable inscribed tablets. After the discovery of the tablets, the contemporaries of the clergyman had no suspicions about the eight mound explorers themselves; the ground was frozen above the tablets, and there were too many people about to think that someone put the slate tablets in the mound during the hasty exploration in loose soil below the frost line. Nevertheless, there was a part of Gass's excavation report that later drew comments from archaeologists. If no one could have planted the tablets at the time they were found, was it possible that someone dug into the mound and buried the tablets before the ground froze? Why did Reverend Gass and his friends find loose dirt and scattered bones?[25]

Others expressed some doubt about the tablets when they examined them closely. Dr. Robert Farquharson, elected president of the Academy the following year, addressed the membership on the importance of the discovery.[26] He began his speech by saying he was astonished and somewhat embarrassed by the discovery, for one of the tablets had some form of phonetic writing, which seemed to prove too much. It seemed almost like a stage trick to have writing suddenly appear in a mound, for he said authorities on American archaeology generally agreed that no ancient race in North America wrote in such letters. Since it appeared to be a discovery made in good faith, it was the duty of the Academy to publish it, so that scientists could judge its merits. The Academy should invite all fair and candid criticism.

He next discussed his impression of the two slate tablets. One was the Calendar stone, marked by twelve signs of the zodiac—none of which duplicated the familiar ones, however. Since no such zodiac was known in the New World, it suggested that there had been some contact with ancient peoples in the Old World. And yet ·he was puzzled to find that by some coincidence the measurements corresponded to modern inches, which suggested a recent origin. He did not elaborate, but my later measurements showed that this slate was 6¾ inches square with two suspension holes ⅜ of an inch in diameter. The circle diameters were set at 2, 3½, 5, and 6¼ inches, the distances between them approximately ¾ of an inch (using a steel compass as scriber to make circles evenly round).

In looking at the slate tablets through a magnifying glass, Dr. Farquharson found that the incisions were uniform and nowhere deep; the original marks of smoothing and polishing present on the surface indicated that the slate had not weathered much. My own examination discovered no traces of weathering.

In reviewing the Cremation Scene tablet, he noted that the upper part bore a mysterious inscription that seemed to have four letters spelling TOWN, although he thought this might be pure fancy on his part (figure 2.7). Below the inscription, he identified symbols representing the sun, moon, and stars, as well as the depiction of a group of Mound Builders holding hands around the altar sacrifice on top of the burial mound.

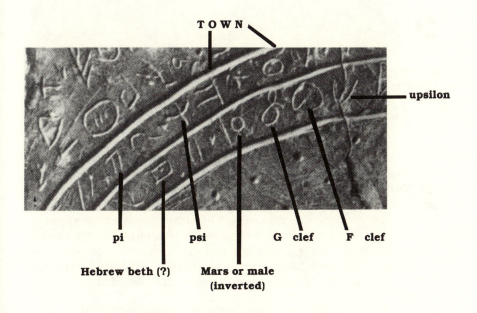

2.7. *Enlarged section of the Cremation Scene inscription. Dr. Farquharson suggested four letters might spell "town" in modern English, although he dismissed it as "pure fancy." Not mentioned by him, other modernisms occur, including nonclassical, lower-case Greek letters and possible musical notation. See also figure 18.1. (Putnam Museum specimen AR-15338)*

The other, split-off half of the same tablet had what was termed the Hunting Scene. Some figures on the margin were broken off and lost. Thirty figures remained, which Dr. Farquharson identified as eight men, four bison, four deer, three birds, three hares, and single examples of a bighorn or Rocky Mountain sheep, a fish, and a prairie wolf. Finally, there were three nondescript animals that might equally represent she-moose, tapirs, or mastodons (figure 2.8).

2.8. Enlarged section of the Hunting Scene. Nondescript animals that Dr. Farquharson thought might represent she-moose, tapirs, or mastodons. (Putnam Museum specimen AR-15339)

Dr. Farquharson favored the mastodon identification, and despite all of his previously expressed cautions and uncertainties, he drew a most startling conclusion for his audience at the Academy. He ended his talk by saying that he believed the mound explorers had made a *bona fide* discovery. They had completed the chain of evidence that finally linked the ancient Mound Builders with Old World culture, written language, and the mastodon. This was wonderful news, the Academy president was cheered by his audience, and his talk was almost immediately published in the *Proceedings.*[27]

The enthusiastic mound diggers had broken through the frozen crust of a burial mound and found loose soil, which was a clear indication of prior disturbance. In the midst of the disturbance in the mound soil, they found two slate tablets wrapped in clay, perhaps destroying a third tablet in their haste. They also missed a concretion with quartz eyes cemented with modern white glue, which was found the next day. The tablets were incised, but the incisions were unweathered. The zodiac was copied from an Old World form and could not be prehistoric; in addition, the circles were laid out in modern inches and common inch fractions. The Davenport Academy *Proceedings* noted that the local members cheered the physician's proclamation of authenticity as genuine Mound Builder relics. It is apparent from later testimony that a few Academy members—doubtless attending this very meeting—knew there was far more to the story.

Where did Dr. Farquharson's well-reasoned cautions originate? They came from Professor Frederic Ward Putnam, one of Harvard's legendary founders of North American archaeological research. A second cousin of the Davenport Putnams, he once came to visit them. The Harvard Peabody Museum photographic archives catalogue P917 contains the notation that Putnam had sent Dr. Farquharson letters on 15 and 22 February 1877 giving "my views in full" on the slate tablets and stating "I think them to be forgeries." Had Farquharson paid closer attention to these two letters, no Davenport conspiracy would have occurred.

Professor Putnam never published a word on either the Davenport forgeries or other archaeological frauds he encountered, apparently believing that publication perpetuated forgeries by giving them publicity. The Putnam letters themselves are lost; no copies survive at Harvard Peabody Museum, just the handwritten photographic notation that Professor Stephen Williams brought to my attention. Dr. Farquharson apparently kept the letters as personal correspondence; they did not become included in the Davenport Putnam Museum archives, according to Janice Hall, who searched for them at my request.

3

WHO WROTE THE TABLETS?

The Davenport Academy acted swiftly and with the greatest propriety. Reverend Gass discovered the unique slate tablets in January 1877, and the following April, encased in plaster and wooden frames, they arrived at the Smithsonian Institution. The initial comments were favorable. The secretary of the Smithsonian, Professor Spenser Baird, wrote that there was every indication of genuineness and that the tablets attracted considerable interest. In a subsequent letter, Baird explained that photographs had been shown informally to some scholars attending the meeting of the National Academy of Sciences, and the preliminary opinions considered the Davenport tablets to be of great antiquity. Among those who offered such opinions was the almost legendary anthropologist, Lewis Henry Morgan.[1]

To make a more formal assessment, Spenser Baird assigned the study of the tablets to an assistant, Dr. E. Foreman. The tablets received a cursory examination, and very soon after Baird's optimistic letter was received, Dr. Foreman's preliminary note arrived. It contained bad news. Foreman wrote that he did not believe the tablets to be ancient. A second communication enclosed Dr. Foreman's nine-page, handwritten report.[2] Parts of this manuscript are of interest because Foreman's initial questions reappeared in the later struggles over the tablets' authenticity.

The doubts about the archaeological context of the slate tablets came from his examination of the mound drawing. The illustrations and text of the excavation report had not yet been published in the *Proceedings of the Davenport Academy*, but Foreman had been sent an advance copy to help him in his study.[3] Mound 3 at the Cook Farm had two burial pits. Illustrations of the southern pit revealed the skeletons in proper anatomical position with the major bones in place; this was the area excavated in 1874. In contrast, the northern pit showed everything in disorder around the area where the tablets had been found (figure 3.1). Foreman noted that one of the bones was stained by contact with copper; however, this bone and its associated copper were not found together in the burial area. He concluded that the northern burial pit had been "thoroughly ransacked" and the relics removed by some person who then put in the tablets for the purpose of deception. The layer of shells had been put back in place and the mound refilled. This accounted for the loose soil that the clergyman and his friends had noticed around the tablets. In short, Dr. Foreman concluded that Reverend Gass unknowingly had excavated a ransacked mound.[4] His conclusion rested upon Jacob Gass's own observations, and it was plain that

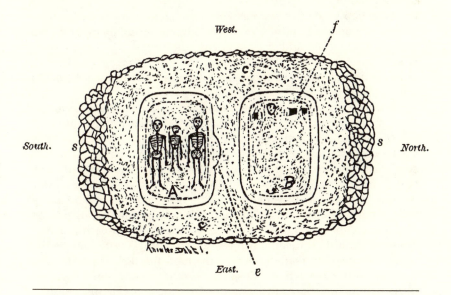

3.1. *Using this illustration given to him in prepublication form by Academy curator Pratt, Dr. Edward Foreman concluded that Burial Pit A (left) had been intact when excavated by Rev. Gass in 1874 because the skeletons were found in proper anatomical position. In contrast, Burial Pit B at right contained loose dirt and human bones were scattered about—Rev. Gass had redug a recent excavation. The tablets were found at location f. (Gass 1877a:92–93)*

the clergyman was not trying to deceive anyone by making false claims that the mound contents were undisturbed. The mound burials had been clearly churned up.

Although Foreman did not mention the fact that the Calendar stone was laid out in inch measurements, he argued that it was of recent origin. The fresh incisions were unweathered. The circles were drawn perfectly round by using the sharp point of a compass, and this explained the central pit in the center of the tablet. He specifically suggested that a steel carpenter's compass had been used for the work.

Furthermore, he attempted to interpret the Cremation and Hunting scenes as influenced by Christianity. This gave them a post-Columbian date, which fitted with the other evidence. The zodiac signs of the crab, scorpion, bow and arrow, and the twins seemed to be represented on the Calendar stone, and the stone's twelve-month zodiac did not conform to the usual native calendar of thirteen moons.

Who had made the tablets? Foreman suggested that some half-breed or trapper might have made them while lounging away a long winter. But he then added a postscript: the engraving of the tablets might have been a harmless pastime, but "the Knavery commences with the introduction of them into a mound centuries old for the purpose of deception."[5]

Such a conclusion, suggesting an act of knavery and no antiquity for the tablets, did not sit easily with two important members of the Davenport Academy. One of them was William Pratt, owner of the Davenport Commercial College and a leading member, who had served continuously in one office or another since the Academy was first formed in 1867.[6] Pratt's real interest was natural history; after election to a term as president in 1880–81, he gave up his business college entirely and became the first full-time curator, a position he held throughout the crisis in the next decade. His most promising assistant was J. Duncan Putnam, eldest and favorite son of the wealthy lawyer who later endowed the museum. Pratt and Duncan Putnam were close friends despite the difference in age of almost thirty years, and the young man bought Pratt a life membership in the Academy, which suggests that the management of the Commercial College had been somewhat neglected for science. Duncan Putnam's primary interest was entomology, and he attended Harvard intermittently as his delicate health would allow. When he died at the early age of twenty-six in 1881, his father, Charles Putnam, absorbed himself in the Academy and Gass's discoveries, which his favorite son had defended in the last years of his life.

Both Pratt and Duncan Putnam were very displeased with Foreman's report, and they sent off letters of criticism to his boss, Spenser Baird, in Washington. They disputed the ransacked, disturbed appearance of the grave where the tablets were found, and they raised a number of technicalities about the positions of artifacts. Foreman had made some minor errors in his disjointed manuscript report—for example, he had written there were four marks scratched on each quadrant of the Calendar stone, when in fact only three marks appear. Foreman's report was a first draft; it should have been held back from the Academy and a more professional rewriting submitted for preliminary review.

When Foreman received the criticisms of his paper, he wrote Duncan Putnam that he did not advise the Academy to print his report but added that he thought the two slate tablets were "fishy" and saw no reason whatever to change his opinion.[7] The word *fishy* was a poor word choice, and like *knavery* it suggested that the Academy was somehow involved in perpetrating relic frauds.

Although Foreman defended his objections to the tablets, Spenser Baird thought that the Smithsonian had committed itself too strongly. Duncan Putnam and Pratt had complained about Foreman's evaluation and said it was hasty and inaccurate. Baird replied: "The criticisms of Dr. Foreman on the tablets are not to be considered of any weight whatever nor as expressing any views which the Smithsonian Institution may be supposed to entertain in regard to them. I do not believe he has read, or at least very carefully, the full history of their discovery; and I have no doubt but that he has been hasty in his conclusions."[8] In fact, the "full history," along with a diagram of the mound, was precisely the evidence Foreman used to point out archaeological disturbance and suggest a ransacked mound. With a friend "at court" supporting the tablets, however, the Academy members felt that the authenticity of the discovery had been confirmed. Had a corrected and somewhat modified report been issued by Foreman, some of the charges later raised would have been clarified from the beginning.

It was so difficult to accept the inscribed tablets that other explanations were used by some to avoid questioning the role of Reverend Gass. One of these alternatives, first raised by Dr. Farquharson in 1877, was the possibility that Mormons had planted the tablets in the mound. (The same suggestion was made by the Reverend Stephen Peet in 1892.)[9] Such a solution to the dilemma cleared local Academy members of any guilt and still allowed the tablets to be rejected as spurious. We may suspect the influence of Foreman's manuscript upon Dr. Farquharson. Unfortunately, the physician soon left Davenport for a position in Des Moines, where he died in 1884, and his cautions were no longer of weight within the Academy. With the publication of the discovery of the tablets in the *Proceedings,* the way was open for extreme, far-ranging views.

Professor Seyffarth of Philadelphia received a copy of volume two of the *Proceedings,* which contained the account of the tablets by Farquharson and others and illustrated the two slate tablets in clear photographs. Seyffarth concluded that *the tablets proved that the primitive inhabitants of North America were not offsprings of monkeys but descendants of Noah.* He dated the Dispersion of Nations in the Old World at 2780 B.C., an event resulting in migrations to America from China, Japan, or Korea prior to the year 1597 B.C.[10] Seyffarth had excavated sites in Europe, first publishing in 1825, and was a very old man in 1881 when he described the Davenport tablets in the biblical context of Noah, the Great Deluge, and the Dispersion. His conclusion was little more than vintage Spanish Conquest theology, such as had been propounded in 1537 by Pope Paul III to justify native civil rights.[11]

Seyffarth's article was promptly published in the *Proceedings of the Davenport Academy* because it provided one line of defense for the slate tablets: they were important, authentic relics. That Seyffarth was totally ignorant of nineteenth-century geology, Paleolithic archaeology, and Darwinian evolution mattered not a whit to the businessmen who were transforming the science academy into social club rooms.

Among various theories about the tablets, only one writer actually claimed a decipherment of the Cremation Scene inscription. John Campbell of Montreal published two articles in leading scientific journals, the *American Antiquarian* and *Transactions of the American Association for the Advancement of Science.*[12] Campbell wrote that Hittite hieroglyphics provided the key to the Davenport slate tablet. It demonstrated, Campbell wrote, the Hittite origin of the Mound Builders. He traced them from the Near East on a course of migration through Siberia to the New World, where they built North American earthworks and founded the Aztec empire. His decipherment of the Davenport tablet was garbled and his commentary obscure. He explained: "We may regard Sataba as justly incurring the penalty of death for murder, but it is hard to say why the maiden Sapoca and Alcaalisca, who was probably the son of Alpi, should have suffered at the same time. The expression . . . would seem to convey the idea that sacrifices were offered on their behalf. . . . "[13] About Campbell's commentary, it is enough to point out that Hittite was not successfully deciphered for another thirty years. Neither Hittite cuneiform nor hieroglyphic scripts remotely resemble the Davenport inscription. That Campbell's attempted translation was so readily published in scientific journals points to the grip that mound speculations had upon scientific inquiry in the 1880s. The editors who approved publication were working in the dark.

Meanwhile, a third attempt was made to interpret the slate tablets. Horatio Rust of Pasadena, California, published an abstract of his findings in the *Proceedings of the American Association for the Advancement of Science.*[14] He reportedly showed photographs of the slate tablets to Dakota Indians, and several of the older men told him that the Cremation Scene tablet did not represent a mound ceremony at all but depicted an earth lodge with a dance held inside on a cold night. The writing was identified by the Indians as ornamental markings without meaning. The Dakota Indians' identification of the burial mound as an earth lodge resolved the Mound Builder problem in an unusual way, as did their elimination of the writing as a meaningful inscription. Yet Rust stood virtually alone in denying that writing was present on the slate tablets. Most observers interpreted the markings as symbolic characters, but the true significance of the inscription remained unknown.

It had been an antiquarian field day. The mysterious tablet writers had been successively identified as modern knaves, early fur traders, Mormons, descendants of Noah, the ancient Hittites who became Aztecs, and finally, ancestors of contemporary native Americans. Some years later there were local rumors that Davenport Academy members hastily scrawled on the slates and buried them to make a fool of the hated preacher. A century later, in 1977, the *Reader's Digest* published an article that identified the Davenport Cremation Scene tablet as the American Rosetta stone.[15] This was based upon the decipherment of 1976 by Professor Barry Fell, who claimed the text was a trilingual inscription left by an international brigade of Egyptians, Libyans, and Phoenicians who visited Iowa thousands of years ago.[16] Who, in fact, had carved the slate tablets?

4

THE LIMESTONE TABLET
AND ELEPHANT PIPES

While antiquarians speculated about the two slate tablets
from Mound 3 at the Cook Farm, the elected officers of the Davenport Academy thought it worthwhile to obtain "certificates" from
the volunteers who excavated under the direction of Reverend Gass.
These certificates are no longer in the files but are mentioned in the
Davenport Academy *Proceedings* of 1877.[1] The purpose was to substantiate the statements published by Reverend Gass; the participants testified under oath that all was true about the accounts of the
discoveries.[2]

The original 1874 excavations at the Cook Farm mounds were
certified by three German-speaking immigrants, including Gass's
brother-in-law, Reverend Borgelt. The more remarkable finds of
slate tablets in Mound 3 were supported by the signatures of seven
other German or Swiss-German ethnics, including several clergymen. Not one of the witnesses on the crew held membership in the
Yankee-dominated Academy, and only one of them, Reverend
Adolph Blumer (another clergyman brother-in-law of Gass), was later elected to Academy membership. The presence of Lutheran
clergymen and theological students gave the excavations an air of
authenticity. As was well known at the time, French clergymen
were making major Paleolithic discoveries in Europe; Davenport
seemed to be a parallel situation. Thus, the Iowa heresay became
"unimpeached statements" during the later defense of the relics in
Science.[3]

It was next decided that prominent Davenport Academy members should witness future amazing discoveries. Some of the Academy Yankees meanwhile encouraged Reverend Gass to try his luck again. For some reason, Gass had overlooked a small mound at the Cook Farm. The Yankees patched up a truce between the tenant and Reverend Gass so that he could return to the scene of his former successes. They arranged matters so that the excavation took place in January 1878, the clergyman's lucky month for excavation, almost exactly a year after the discovery of the slate tablets. Reverend Gass was accompanied by two Yankees to give respectability to the prospective findings. One of them, Charles Harrison, later served as both vice president and president of the Academy. The other man, John Hume, served in a variety of less important offices.

These three men arrived at the Cook Farm in January 1878 and extended scientific inquiries by smashing up the previously overlooked Mound 11, now frozen to a depth of seven or eight inches. Success soon rewarded their enterprise. They encountered a pile of limestones, which they apparently threw to one side in their haste to see what treasures might be concealed within (figure 4.1). For this reason, there remains uncertainty about the shape of the limestone pile found inside the mound. Gass wrote no report, leaving the

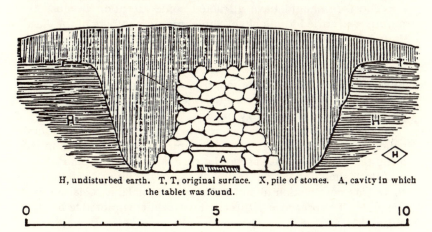

H, undisturbed earth.   T, T, original surface.   X, pile of stones.   A, cavity in which
the tablet was found.

0   5   10

4.1. *Crypt of the Iowa Mound Builder. In this drawing, Harrison resurrected the hasty excavation of Mound 11, Cook Farm. Accounts vary as to the shape of the rock cairn—a pyramid or, as shown, a flat-topped altar. (Approximate scale in feet added to original drawing.) (Harrison 1880:222)*

matter up to Harrison, who described the limestones as forming an "altar."[4] Local tradition described the pile as a "pyramid."[5]

Demolishing the pyramid or altar, the three enthusiasts found a hole or small chamber beneath the limestones. Looking inside, the excavators were startled to see the red face of a Mound Builder staring back at them.

The face was painted on a limestone tablet, bright and clean, unmarked by weathering or other signs of antiquity. No dirt or debris lay upon it. This fact raised legitimate suspicions about the circumstances of discovery. Archaeologists later wondered whether such a find could be ancient.[6]

This tablet, despite the appearance of recent origin, had elements of design and association that tied together the earlier discoveries. Outlined with grooves, the complete Indian figure was painted with a mineral pigment, red ochre, sometimes found in the mounds. This Mound Builder, crudely drawn, was shown sitting on a portrayal of the sun with a face and rays. In one hand the Mound Builder held a bow; the other hand seems to have been incompletely made, or else there was a stone insert that was lost (figure 4.2). This specimen received rough handling, as will be explained, and so either explanation might serve.

The face should have attracted some attention because the mouth was curled into a slight smile; many members of the Academy didn't know enough at the time to laugh along with the Mound Builder. Above this figure appeared representations of a copper axe and two platform effigy pipes—bird effigies very similar to the ones Reverend Gass had actually found in the Cook Farm mounds and elsewhere. There were small quartz crystals attached with white glue on the eyes of the effigy pipes.

The excavation report by Harrison also mentioned a large conch shell filled with red ochre, the mineral pigment used in coloring the tablet. With it appeared a very large and fine quartz crystal.[7] Both shell and crystal rested on top of the limestone tablet, so there was no question about the quartz crystal's association with the tablet. The presence of this crystal was later rumored to be proof of fraud.[8]

The quartz-crystal eyes adorning the effigy pipes on the limestone tablet exactly resembled those on the strange concretion found in the back dirt of Mound 3 during the discovery of the slate tablets. This provided additional linkage of the various discoveries. They were either all genuine or all spurious.

Mound 11 was gutted with great haste during a single January

4.2. The Iowa Mound Builder with a Mona Lisa smile. The limestone tablet is 7 by 12 inches and 1½ inches thick. This early photograph shows that both effigy pipes depicted at the top had quartz
eyes that were glued on with white cement; the eyes were subsequently lost. (Putnam Museum specimen AR-15342, published in
PDANS 2:pl. 8)

day. The limestone altar or pyramid was destroyed before its shape was determined, and the initially "bright and clean" limestone tablet was battered during its speedy removal. It broke into eight fragments, and two edge pieces were never recovered. (Even in the Academy, specimens did not always receive careful handling. After the limestone tablet was photographed for publication, the quartz eyes fell out and were lost. The quartz eyes on the concretion found in the back dirt of Mound 3 became unglued and disappeared. Later, an elephant pipe, the first of its kind ever found, was dropped and broken while casting a duplicate for exhibition. At least two other pipes were broken through careless handling during study, and other specimens were battered and chipped.[9] In later years, through the lack of security, specimens were stolen for private collections.)

The excavation of Mound 11 and the battering of the limestone tablet showed a lack of skill conspicuous even for the 1870s. The uniqueness and novelty of the growing number of finds was proving to be almost embarrassing. They seemed to lack antiquity, to judge from their fresh appearance. Nevertheless, supporters of the research could plausibly argue that no taint of scandal could be attributed to the finders, who were men working in good faith. Charles Putnam later defended Harrison, Hume, and Gass by writing that they were "well and favorably known in the community . . . and the well attested facts connected therewith establish, beyond reasonable doubt, that whether more or less ancient, the tablet was deposited at the making of the mound."[10]

Meanwhile, fresh discoveries fascinated the followers of the amazing Davenport tablets. During an exploring trip to Louisa County, south of Davenport, Reverend Gass heard about an unusual pipe owned by a farmer. Following up this story, Gass recognized that the effigy of an elephant made it unique. The farmer refused to sell the remarkable object, insisting that he used it for smoking. Gass borrowed it in order to have casts and photographs made at the Academy. The original was accidentally dropped and broken, and since repairs made it worthless for smoking, the Academy paid a small sum and purchased the elephant pipe to appease the owner. As an illustration of the vagueness that surrounded the purchase, the published reports variously claim the amount paid the farmer was three, four, or five dollars.[11]

The account describing the acquisition of the unique pipe that portrayed a tuskless mammoth or mastodon states that a German farmer, Peter Mare, found the pipe in a cornfield. The catalogue entry gives the date of his discovery as March 1873. He attached no particular importance to the unusual object and occasionally smoked it. Upon leaving for Kansas, Mare gave it to his brother-in-law, the owner when Gass obtained it for the Academy. It was a straightforward story.[12]

A single example of such an unusual effigy pipe naturally raised a question about its authenticity. Since it had been a surface find and did not come from a documented excavation, some wondered if it was genuine and others questioned whether the artist had really intended to portray a mammoth or mastodon. These doubts were soon dispelled by a second find: a more realistic elephant pipe (portraying the beast with a shaggy wool coat) that came from a documented excavation (figure 4.3). This find was made in 1880 during an excavation of a mound in Louisa County near the cornfield where the first elephant pipe came to light. Reverend Adolph Blumer—a clergyman from Geneseo, Illinois—had been in the crew of Germans that found the slate tablets. He and his brother-in-law, Jacob Gass, were clearing the mound when, at a depth of six feet, Blumer found and removed the elephant pipe with his own hands.

Reverend Blumer wrote up his report of the find for publication in the Davenport Academy *Proceedings*.[13] The upper layer of the mound, eighteen inches of clay, covered a middle layer of unbroken,

4.3. This second elephant effigy, with the shaggy coat, answered questions asked about the first elephant, such as Was the Pleistocene woolly mammoth depicted? (Putnam Museum specimen AR-14778)

fire-hardened clay some three feet thick. Beneath this, in a layer of
ash, the remarkable pipe had appeared. The report made it clear
that the elephant pipe had been sealed in the mound by undisturbed layers of clay, and accordingly, the remarkable discovery
made by two clergymen conclusively demonstrated that the Mound
Builders had known mammoth or mastodon. The only uncertainty
was which kind of elephant, because the new find was portrayed as
tuskless. Every other doubt was answered. There were additional
witnesses to the discovery, since several local farmers and the son of
the landowner helped out during the mound exploration. Every favorable circumstance demonstrated authenticity—a previous find
of a cruder example, reliable excavators who were clergy, supporting witnesses, and a well-sealed mound deposit that would have
made some intrusive fraud conspicuous. Reports of this and other
discoveries convinced most antiquarians that the elephant pipes
and the tablets must be genuine.[14]

The wealthy lawyer, Charles Putnam, now gave Reverend Gass
funds to explore more widely and also purchase interesting specimens from amateur collections. Gass applied himself on an almost
full-time basis with his characteristic vigor, angering many of his
parishioners by abandoning some of his duties at the First Lutheran
Church. Gass traveled far and wide, digging up specimens and also
buying them, and in this way he amassed a sizeable collection of
effigy pipes for the Academy that were unique in variety and form—
unmatched by any other collection.[15] He also found at least five
other mysterious stone tablets with inscriptions, although for some
reason these discoveries were not publicized or sent off to the
Smithsonian Institution for an independent appraisal.[16]

Stories began to circulate about Reverend Gass in the Davenport area. His many enemies questioned his activities. His relic-
trading wheeling and dealing antagonized others (see chapter 7). By
1882 his long-suffering Lutheran parish had had enough of his antiquarian ventures. In January 1883 Gass also resigned as a trustee
of the Davenport Academy and left for a new parish at Postville in
northern Iowa. He soon gathered together a sizeable enough congregation of German-speaking Lutherans to build one of the largest
churches in the area, and for a time he prospered as a clergyman,
until new enemies forced his retirement. Meanwhile, Reverend Gass
became a legend in the Davenport Academy. After he left town,
some people still talked about him in a puzzled way—was he a fool,
a rascal and forger, or the Heinrich Schliemann of North America,
an archaeological explorer whose finds had changed history?

5

THE STORM BREAKS

Professional archaeologists, who were very few in number, viewed the dramatic Davenport discoveries with considerable caution. In the *American Naturalist,* Otis T. Mason went so far as to warn the Davenport Academy against the dangers of being "duped by some wag."[1] Various other comments and rejoinders appeared in that journal and others. Major John Wesley Powell continued to be deeply concerned about the growing number of archaeological frauds and the unfounded speculations these frauds generated about the lost race of Mound Builders. He specifically cautioned against "enthusiastic theorists" and "blind zeal" leading to fantasies about ancient civilizations coming to North America from the Old World. His warning about mound mythology was published in his introduction to the *Bureau of Ethnology Report* of 1883.[2] The context was his introductory comments about a research article written by a staff member, Henry Henshaw, which appeared later in the same volume under the title "Animal Carvings from Mounds of the Mississippi Valley."[3] In the course of his study, the author attacked the Davenport Academy specimens and opened a raging controversy. Instead of casting doubt on the two elephant pipes, it indirectly made them even more famous.

Henshaw's study examined the identification of animals carved on the effigy platform pipes found in the burial mounds. It had been reported that bird-effigy pipes represented parrots typical of Central America. If true, these effigies suggested that the Mound Builders had migrated into North America from the south, bringing a higher civilization than tribalism with them, a conclusion drawn in the famous 1848 Smithsonian report by Squire and Davis.[4] By training, Henshaw was an ornithologist, and his identification of bird effigies carried weight.

In his report, Henshaw concluded that the effigy birds on the pipes were frequently too stylized to identify the species. Those effigies more realistically portrayed represented bird species that were local to the area in which the pipe had been found. According to Henshaw, the so-called parrot pipes were misidentifications, and his conclusion that indigenous species were represented on mound art provided no support for the lost race theories being used to explain the prehistoric earthworks as constructions by southern invaders.

The two unique elephant pipes from Davenport represented a special problem because no techniques had yet been developed to determine the ages of prehistoric artifacts or animals, and it was unclear when the Pleistocene elephants became extinct. However, he added, there was no proof that the Mound Builders were contemporaneous with the mastodon. The elephant pipes and the crudely drawn, possible elephant on the Hunting Scene slate tablet raised a more serious issue. Were the artifacts genuine? Henshaw wrote that it raised suspicion that one man found all of these artifacts, particularly when equally active mound explorers in the area had failed to find anything like them.

> Bearing in mind the many attempts at archaeological frauds that recent years have brought to light, archaeologists have a right to demand that objects which afford a basis for such important deductions as the coeval life of the Mound-Builder and the mastodon should be above the slightest suspicion not only in respect to their resemblances, but as regards the circumstances of discovery. If they are not above suspicion, the science of archaeology can better afford to wait for further and more certain evidence than to commit itself to theories which may prove stumbling-blocks to truth until that indefinite time when future investigations shall show their illusory nature.[5]

The reference to fraud was reinforced by a personal attack upon the discoverer of the relics. Henshaw wrote that a "remarkable archaeologic instinct" and a "divining rod" led the same man to the slate tablets.

The repeated allusion to fraud was not reinforced by any discussion of evidence, and accordingly his remarks were taken as a personal attack upon the integrity of Reverend Gass, even though Henshaw did not mention Gass by name. The Iowa clergyman had not used a *divining rod;* there was a stronger case to be made that good luck and hard work led the clergyman to his famous discoveries rather than the disparaging *remarkable archaeologic instinct.* The handful of professional archaeologists read such remarks with glee, but the amateur antiquarians around the country were upset by the dismissal of evidence without the presentation of proof. Henshaw had attempted to shift the burden of proving innocence upon the Davenport Academy, but this attempt initially failed because he did not substantiate his charges. Many members of the Davenport Academy considered Henshaw's remarks to be no more than "insinuations and slanders."[6] Locally, the Smithsonian experts were damned as "relic sharps," a demeaning term later printed about them in connection with the controversy.[7]

Although the publication date of Henshaw's attack was 1883, it was not circulated to the public until late the next year. When the report reached the Davenport Academy, it was unexpected and caused considerable commotion. A special meeting of the membership was called into session, and the prominent attorney Charles Putnam was chosen to lead the defense and to prepare a reply to the Smithsonian charges of fraud (figure 5.1).

Charles Putnam threw his whole energy into the project because he believed that Henshaw's charges were outrageous and debased the scientific work of the Academy. Why had the attack been made? Putnam suspected a plot stemming from the Smithsonian that was intended to destroy the Academy as a research institution. He carefully read Henshaw's study and noted inconsistencies.

Charles Putnam was a very able lawyer, and his lengthy written defense had a courtroom ring to it. His strategy was to prove, as if to a trial jury, that there was *reasonable doubt* about the Smithsonian charges. To establish reasonable doubt, he fired off a barrage of commentary filled with inconsequential details in order to demonstrate that the Smithsonian experts were hasty, inaccurate, and not competent to judge the origin of the tablets and elephant pipes. As one example, Henshaw had written that the discoverer had used a *divining rod* to find the elephant pipes, and this led him to the tablets—a reversal of the published dates in the sequence of excavation. This correctly demonstrated that Henshaw was relatively unfamiliar with the published reports about the discoveries and raised a question about his competence to judge the matter.

Another illustration of Putnam's legal skills was his demonstration that Henry Henshaw was guilty of sloppy scholarship because his attack described the pipe carvings as *elephants without tails.*

5.1.   *Charles E. Putnam (1825–1887) successfully used the legal
defense of* reasonable doubt *to disarm every criticism. A complex,
talented man, he endowed the Academy with a substantial part of
his great wealth, ensuring its survival as a major regional museum, now named for him. (Putnam Museum)*

Putnam cleverly showed that Henshaw had used as his source an
inaccurate drawing from an unnamed "eastern magazine" rather
than the more accurate publication in the Davenport Academy *Proceedings.* Putnam triumphantly reprinted the original illustrations
with the elephant tails prominently in view, which made Henshaw
appear to be a prejudiced liar whose opinions were worthless (figure
5.2). The lawyer also questioned the intrusion of the Bureau of
Ethnology into prehistoric studies, branding the research an example of Major Powell's "hobby" carried out at government expense
by his henchmen in Washington.

    Putnam's defense first appeared in a printed report of 1885, and
the Davenport Academy sent out free copies to every science academy in the country, with additional copies for major journals and
prominent scholars.[8] In response, the Davenport Academy was in-
undated with correspondence from antiquarians, most of it highly

5.2.   Elephant tales. Henshaw's critique erred in saying the two
Iowa elephant effigies lacked tails, leaving the way open for Putnam's rebuttal, which provided this illustration with the elephant
tails prominently displayed. (Putnam 1885 and 1886:271)

favorable to Putnam's legalistic defense. This correspondence was
added as an appendix of ninety-seven pages to the second edition
issued in the Davenport Academy *Proceedings* (1886).[9] This appendix was also issued as a separate monograph and sent out to anyone
interested in reading about the Mound Builders. So many free copies were printed that it was still available at the museum until the
early 1970s, when the supply was finally exhausted.[10]

The defense of the specimens began with the bitter note that it was a "vindication of the elephant pipes and inscribed tablets . . . from the accusations of the Bureau of Ethnology of the Smithsonian Institution." It is an interesting document, and taken by itself, without reference to all of the facts, it is surprisingly convincing. Even today, one gains the impression that Smithsonian experts were in fact distorting evidence and plotting to destroy the amateur research academies. A selection from the correspondence reprinted in 1886 demonstrates Putnam's remarkable success in arousing the emotions over Smithsonian involvement in the Mound Builder question:

> I fear there has been some hasty dogmatizing in Washington. *Prof. Alexander Winchell, Ann Arbor, Michigan*

> They had no warrant for their attack and you were justified throughout in exposing them. *S. A. Miller, Cincinnati, Ohio*

> You certainly have literally annihilated Henshaw, and it is to be hoped that he will at once retire into the obscurity from which Major Powell dragged him forth, and that his like may never again be seen in the land. *Rev. J. P. MacLean, Hamilton, Ohio*

> Your ably-written paper has the effect of a thunderbolt upon the stagnant insinuations of Mr. Henshaw. It purifies the cause of ethnology. *A. C. Webber, Decatur, Illinois*

> The defense of Mr. Gass is the defense of all private investigators. *W. A. Chapman, Okolona, Arkansas*

> Nor is Major Powell exempt from censure in permitting this mass of cruel insinuations to go forth. *S. A. Brinkley, Alexandria, Ohio*

> It is to be wondered at that so eager attacks are undertaken as to the authenticity of relics without any inspection of the things themselves. *Max Uhle, Dresden, Prussia*

> The elephant pipes, which have elicited so much criticism, I consider as genuine as the most undoubted specimens in the museum. Subjected to the sharpest tests, they pass successfully. *Dr. Willis de Hass, Washington, D.C.*

> I consider it a triumphant refutation of the accusations of
> Mr. Henshaw and absurd theories of the Bureau of Ethnology in
> the Smithsonian Institution. *Dr. Edwin Hamilton Davis, New
> York*[11]

Much of the correspondence was written by amateur collectors,
but some well-recognized scholars defended the relics and agreed
with Putnam's charges. Dr. Davis, for instance, was coauthor of the
famous 1848 report by Squire and Davis published as the first volume of the *Smithsonian Contributions to Knowledge,* a study that
distinguished between Mound Builders and Indians. Max Uhle of
Prussia later worked with Professor A. L. Kroeber of the University
of California, Berkeley, on Peruvian archaeology, becoming a recognized specialist in that study.[12]

The masterly lawyer's defense evaded the issue of the genuineness of the specimens by publicly proclaiming the integrity of Gass
and other members of the Academy and then questioning the motives of Henshaw. Putnam had in fact succeeded in turning the
argument around, so that the insinuations made about Reverend
Gass were now made about the Smithsonian. With this approach,
he had obtained the sympathy of gentlemen-antiquarians around
the country, of many scholars, and even of various scientific
journals.[13]

The editor of the *American Antiquarian,* Stephen Peet, wrote
that Henshaw's article was pretentious and groundless, and designed to arouse prejudice against the Bureau of Ethnology. In the
Pacific Science Monthly, Dr. Stephen Bowers expressed his opinions colloquially, writing that "Mr. Putnam replies in an incisive
way that will doubtless cause the Washington relic sharps to look a
'leedle out.'" The July 1885 issue of the *American Naturalist*
favored the Davenport Academy in the dispute: "The article is racy
reading, and incidentally gives strong arguments against the desire
for centralization in science shown in certain quarters. It will be
found impossible to concentrate all science in one clique or city."
The *American Journal of Science* of May 1885 presented its
readers with a lengthy summary of Putnam's defense, quoting him
directly. There was no editorial comment, and his conclusions stood
without rebuttal.[14]

The prestigious English periodical *Nature* took up the question
in its April 1885 issue. After discussing the scientific questions involved, it concluded, "The whole subject is one of extraordinary
interest, and Mr. Putnam's statement, vouched as it is by a formal

resolution of the Davenport Academy, must play an important part in any subsequent discussion as to the value attached to these remains, which, if authentic, are acknowledged to have much influence on the final settlement of the question as to who the Moundbuilders were."[15]

The lawyer, Charles Putnam, rested his case. *In 1885 the jury of scholars and antiquarians found the Smithsonian guilty of persecuting amateurs and making unjustifiable accusations.* In a courtroom such a victory would have been final. But it was not a courtroom, it was a scholarly debate.

6

CIRCUMSTANCES OF DISCOVERY

To those unaware of the intricacies of the problem, Putnam's defense, together with his compilation of supporting letters and journal reviews, conclusively restored the authenticity of the specimens. The longer 1886 version appeared at a difficult time, however. Some strange transactions and relic forgeries attributed to Reverend Gass were publicized in the *American Antiquarian*. Meanwhile, the membership of the Davenport Academy became divided over the authenticity of the unique artifacts. The most immediate emergency, however, was raised by questions and statements made by Cyrus Thomas. He published his objections in *Science* and publicly argued that the tablets and pipes were frauds.

Professor Cyrus Thomas, a colleague of Henshaw and the director of archaeological explorations for the Bureau of Ethnology, had entertained some suspicions of archaeological fraud since the year 1882. As far as he was concerned, the turning point in his investigation came from private information received from a prominent member of the Davenport Academy.

One of the field assistants working for Cyrus Thomas was a former Civil War officer in the Union Army, Colonel P. W. Norris, who worked on mound explorations in a number of states. He had excavated two sites in northeastern Iowa and then visited Davenport, where he met A. S. Tiffany, one of the original organizers of the Academy in 1867 (figure 6.1).[1] Tiffany was not well educated but had a wide range of intellectual interests, including local archaeology, and he had published five very brief notes on his own excavations or specimens.[2] Tiffany told Norris that both the lime-

6.1.   *A. S. Tiffany. One of the three original founders of the Davenport Academy, he became a central figure in the disputes over the
authenticity of the relics and was later expelled from
membership. (Putnam Museum)*

stone tablet and the two elephant pipes were frauds. Either at the
suggestion of Cyrus Thomas or Norris himself, Tiffany wrote a letter
to Norris that expressed his views.[3] This letter, discussed in chapter
8, led to a very bitter debate and to hearings that expelled Tiffany
and his defender, Dr. Lindley, from Academy membership.

Undoubtedly, Henry Henshaw had talked with Norris about the
Davenport specimens found by Reverend Gass before writing up his
opinion about them. The letter written by Tiffany to Norris was
dated October 1882, and it was kept by Cyrus Thomas. By this time
a number of Smithsonian archaeologists were becoming knowledgeable about the Davenport Academy—Foreman, Norris, Henshaw, Thomas, and the director of the Bureau of American Ethnology, Major Powell.

The blast against the Smithsonian, so widely circulated by
Charles Putnam, apparently forced the hand of Cyrus Thomas, for
the charges were serious—slandering Reverend Gass, attempting to
destroy private research, and attempting to have the government
run everything. It also did not look good to have a lawyer claim that

the Smithsonian was inaccurate and hasty in its studies.

Cyrus Thomas chose to respond to Putnam in a nongovernment publication and published a note in the prestigious journal *Science* in December 1885. He did not discuss the charges leveled against the Smithsonian but was concerned with the scientific issue alone— were the unique Davenport specimens actually frauds?[4]

The article was concerned with the discovery of the limestone tablet. By a strange coincidence that tablet had both a Roman numeral VIII and an Arabic number 8, both of which corresponded with the year it was found—1878 (figure 6.2). Since Arabic numbers were not commonly used in Europe until long after the Spanish conquest of Mexico, the presence of this figure confirmed that the tablet was not prehistoric. In addition, circumstantial evidence showed that the tablet had only been in the ground for a short time before it was dug up by Reverend Gass. The original excavation report noted that the removal of a rough limestone slab of rock revealed a cavity beneath it, and the engraved tablet was *suddenly exposed* to view in this hole. In order to be certain of this fact, Cyrus Thomas wrote to the curator, William Pratt, who in turn asked Charles Harrison about it. The cavity, Pratt wrote, *contained scarcely any dirt.* Thomas continued his discussion by saying that a centuries-old monument made of stone rubble and loose dirt would fill up any empty hole beneath it. He then quoted from Tiffany's letter, which stated that the red paint on the tablet was bright

6.2. *Curious Roman and Arabic eights (enlarged section of the Mound Builder tablet). (Putnam Museum specimen AR-15342)*

and clean when it was found in the hole. He concluded by giving Tiffany's view that both the tablet and the elephant pipes were frauds that had been planted to deceive Reverend Gass.

Rejecting the limestone tablet and the elephant pipes, Cyrus Thomas continued the attack. In the next issue of *Science*, published in January 1886, he described features of the two slate tablets "calculated to arouse suspicion."[5] For example, the inscription on the Cremation Scene tablet had among the various characters three examples of Arabic 8s, like the one found on the limestone tablet. An animal-like concretion with quartz-inset eyes was later found in the back dirt from the excavation of Mound 3 where the slate tablets were found. Quartz eyes were also found glued to the limestone tablet from Mound 11. Thomas concluded that the figure 8s, other symbolism, and the quartz-inset eyes linked together the limestone and slate tablets from the excavations of 1877 and 1878: "It is thus almost impossible to avoid the conclusion that all must stand or fall together."[6]

He next raised the matter first observed in Foreman's examination of the evidence. The burial area in the southern half of Mound 3, excavated in 1874, had undisturbed burials, in contrast to the disorder Gass encountered in the northern half of the mound when he found the slate tablets in 1877. The loose soil and disarray Gass observed implied that someone had placed the tablets in the mound for the clergyman to find.

There was a final question that had troubled many people. Who would know enough about ancient languages in the Davenport area to forge a fairly lengthy inscription? The fact that no authorities on ancient languages lived in Davenport strongly suggested that the inscription must be genuine. This argument was strengthened by the difficulty that scholars were having in deciphering the message. Scripts from several languages were present, and no agreement existed as to the meaning. One would think a forged message would tell some clear and translatable story. To such arguments Thomas provided an intriguing answer. In the 1872 edition of *Webster's Unabridged Dictionary*, on page 1766, the letters of the various Old World alphabets were illustrated. Thomas suggested that the resemblance of letters from this page to examples found on the inscriptions "in most cases is very strong. The reader can make the comparison for himself."[7] As for the Calendar tablet, page 1704 of the dictionary displayed the illustration of a zodiac very similar to it, with four concentric circles and twelve signs. Such a dictionary, in print only five years at the time the slate tablets were found, would be such a ready source that no one would have to know anything about ancient languages to make an inscription (figure 6.3).

These two articles were read by Charles Putnam, who became very angry. Within two weeks of reviewing the exposé, Putnam had prepared his lawyer's brief in support of the artifacts and sent it off to *Science,* where it was published in early February 1886.[8] Putnam's opening paragraph belittled Cyrus Thomas: "Probably no writer ever before set out to prepare a piece of 'destructive criticism' with so frank a confession of his disqualification for the task." Regarding the curious resemblance between the inscribed tablets and the zodiac and alphabets from *Webster's Dictionary,* Putnam indignantly replied: "These are fair specimens of the arguments by which Professor Thomas attempts to controvert the unimpeached statements of the discoverers. The resemblances indicated are so trivial and purely fanciful as to scarcely attain the level of serious criticism." Putnam had an equally biting response to the suspicion voiced by Thomas that, because it was free of dirt, the limestone tablet had been recently placed in the hole: "Apparently no good reason can be given why a vault so protected from above, as well as at the sides, could not remain empty for ages."[9]

The lawyer then discussed the letter written by Tiffany to the Smithsonian, for he had obtained a copy of the original by somewhat devious means. He discredited the letter by stating that Cyrus Thomas had not quoted from it exactly but had altered the text four times. Thomas had garbled the letter, he argued, and its use was therefore unfair. The lawyer raised a curious challenge, for he called upon Thomas to publish the letter *verbatim.* He explained that if Thomas did publish the actual letter, it "would not only destroy its value as authority, but would subject Professor Thomas himself to censure in resorting to such sources for scientific material." He then gave a final challenge by writing, "Apparently our Washington friends are so anxious to condemn, they are afraid to investigate."[10]

When Putnam's charges against Cyrus Thomas and Tiffany appeared in early February, Thomas became so angry that he immediately wrote a reply, which was published the same month in *Science.* This was his third article on the affair in that journal.[11] His first objection dealt with a reference by Putnam to the controversial Grave Creek tablet, which he had used to establish the authenticity of the Davenport tablets. Thomas pointed out that archaeologists had generally rejected the Grave Creek specimen as spurious. He next repeated the doubts he had expressed about the position of the

6.3. *The Calendar stone is here shown with a superimposed zodiac from a modern* Webster's *Dictionary, rotated for the best fit. The familiar zodiac signs are not ancient but developed in post-Columbian times. The improvised symbolism on the tablet copied some of these signs directly, which betrays a modern origin. Arrows point to incisions that seem to record two significant dates: in Scorpio, November 5, a good time to put the slates into the mound before the ground froze, and in Aries, April 5, a nice spring day for relic hunting when it was anticipated that Reverend Gass could be steered to redig Mound 3. If this interpretation is correct, these marks indicate that a prank was intended without meaning to fool anyone for very long.* (Putnam Museum specimen AR-15341 and Webster's New World Dictionary of the American Language, College Edition [1967]:1700)

limestone tablet in an unfilled hole. In reviewing this reply by Thomas, one may note that he did not directly confront two of Putnam's major challenges. Although he defended Tiffany against the charge of illiteracy, he did not publish an accurate, *verbatim* copy of the letter itself. Nor did he accept the invitation to visit Davenport and inspect the specimens themselves. He somewhat weakly wrote, "If this evidence leads to the conclusion that these relics are modern productions, as I believe it does, there is no necessity for the present of 'further investigation.'"[12] Thus, by his refusal to examine the relics and talk to Academy members, Cyrus Thomas kept the affair open. Putnam was able to ask repeatedly the same damaging questions: Why did the experts in Washington condemn the specimens without making a firsthand investigation in the Davenport area? Why didn't they come? What was the ulterior motive of the Smithsonian?

7

The Trials of Jacob Gass

At the time of the Thomas-Putnam exchange in *Science,* some scholars reversed their previously favorable position and became convinced of the fraud. Among the most prominent of this group was the Reverend Stephen Peet of Clinton, Wisconsin, who made his living as a local clergyman and was the editor of the *American Antiquarian.* He previously had published favorable comments on the unique specimens and had even been cited in Putnam's 1886 version of the vindication of the relics. Peet had written in the *American Antiquarian* that Henshaw's attack was pretentious and groundless.[1] As more information became available, Peet reversed his position and published some highly damning testimony about the affairs of Reverend Jacob Gass and other suspicious circumstances surrounding the discoveries. Public attention had begun to shift from the unfortunate Henshaw to the explorer Gass.

In the January 1886 issue of the *American Antiquarian,* Stephen Peet dropped a bombshell with his editorial entitled "Are the Davenport Tablets Frauds?"[2] It was an eleven-page discussion, with illustrations of anomalies in the inscriptions and diagrams from the original excavation reports. Peet argued that the tablets appeared in a disturbed archaeological context and should be considered intrusive. The excavation reports themselves provided "evidence that deception has been practiced and that 'a plant' has been perpetrated." He concluded his editorial with an intriguing statement about the number of inscribed tablets found by Gass. In addition to the two slate and single limestone tablets found at the Cook Farm, the clergyman had, through some remarkable coincidence, discovered *five other tablets.* These came from a creek bed some twenty-two miles west of Davenport and were very briefly mentioned in a note in the *Proceedings,* unaccompanied by any illustrations. Peet emphasized that he was ready to defend Gass against any attacks on his character and reputation. Yet the fact that so many inscribed tablets had been found raised the question whether some unknown person was planting tablets in the vicinity of Davenport. He wrote that the discoveries were too frequent to be accepted as genuine.[3]

In light of the controversy, it is indeed strange that the discovery of five additional tablets remained so obscure. The largest was left in place in the creek bed, but several were brought back by Gass and given to the museum.[4] I made a search of the museum collection in 1969 and could find no trace of them, and they were not listed in the catalog. I presume they were such obvious fakes that someone quietly threw them away. It would have been interesting to compare the five tablets with the three from the Cook Farm to see if there were parallel details.

When Peet's editorial appeared, the Davenport Academy's curator, William Pratt, angrily replied to the charges in the next month's issue of the *American Antiquarian.*[5] His article, "The Davenport Tablets Genuine," condemned Peet for seeking to create suspicion about the "commonplace" circumstances of discovery. He covered some of the same arguments that Putnam had repeatedly brought up in the defense, and then concluded with provocations: "*Whence* this desperate and blind eagerness to impeach the genuineness of these particular specimens? What are the considerations which prompt such reckless and ill-considered efforts . . . to arouse suspicion and manufacture public opinion?"[6] In short, Pratt questioned the motives and scientific judgment of the editor. Was there indeed a widespread plot against the Academy?

The reply to the curator appeared in the March issue of the *American Antiquarian.* Peet, in a new editorial entitled "The Points Involved," reiterated his previous conclusions and dismissed the charges with the comment that "the method of argument which the writer uses is not one which we admire." He then published some incredible letters and a rejoinder by an amateur, A. F. Berlin, which conclusively demonstrated that Gass had traded fraudulent relics to a private collector.[7]

To understand the impact of the new charges, it should be stated that part of Putnam's defense rested upon the character of Reverend Gass as a man above suspicion:

> The principal discoverer of the inscribed tablets belonged to this
> select circle of voluntary workers, and that, in his own home, his
> word was beyond question and his character above reproach. In
> this connection it may properly be stated that Mr. Gass, who, as
> the discoverer of the unique relics, is assailed by Mr. Henshaw, is
> now preaching to a congregation at Postville, in Northern Iowa,
> where he is, as he everywhere has been, highly esteemed by his
> people. He is a good classical scholar, well grounded in Hebrew,
> but with a decided scientific bent of mind, which accounts for
> his perseverance and enthusiasm in these archaeological ex-
> plorations. It would seem that his fine abilities, extensive attain-
> ments, high social position, and spotless character should have
> shielded him from attack; and if, peradventure, it ever falls to
> the lot of his assailants to themselves encounter "destructive
> criticism," it will then serve them in good stead should they be
> able to confront it with as clean a record.[8]

These words appeared in the vindication of the specimens that Putnam circulated through science academies around the country in
1885 and reprinted in 1886. It was a wonderful testimonial, but was
it true? A relic collector in Pennsylvania, A. F. Berlin, read Putnam's
defense with amazement and then wrote a heated reply to the
American Antiquarian, which was published with documents.[9]

Was Gass a learned man of letters? Berlin, who published some
correspondence by Gass, "corrected the spelling" before it appeared in print. Berlin's purpose was to discuss an 1881 transaction
in which Gass sent clearly fraudulent specimens to H. C. Stevens of
Oregon, three years before Henshaw had published his suspicions.
Berlin is convincing. He had possession of the Gass correspondence
and the frauds themselves. Reverend Jacob Gass had a sideline
business selling relics to out-of-state collectors. Since genuine specimens were rare and became the property of the Davenport Academy, Gass either purchased or manufactured phony relics for his
mail-order business.

Berlin described some of the specimens that Gass had sold out
of state. One was a pipe-shaped object made from white marble and
covered with lead paint. Another was an effigy pipe representing the
neck and head of a bird—it had been hastily made, and the marks of
a steel file were still visible on it. Oblong pieces of red shale labeled
"aboriginal money from Illinois" and a flat, oblong object called a
"sacrificial plate" were equally suspicious.[10] In order to verify his
own conclusions, Berlin shrewdly sent the specimens purchased
from Gass to the Smithsonian to be identified, so that it would not

be his unsupported word as to their nature. In the Berlin correspondence that Putnam compiled at the Academy, there is a copy of
the letter that Cyrus Thomas wrote to Berlin on 21 December 1885.
He said, in part, "I have no doubt that all but one, the one you name
'a sacrificial plate' are frauds. . . . I have always been inclined to
think Mr. Gass straight, but there can be no excuse for a man who
has had any experience with mound relics putting off such specimens as these as genuine."[11]

The amateurs of that day were pillaging archaeological sites
and then trading off the less interesting specimens to other collectors. Frauds were frequently introduced into this barter system.
The particular lot that Berlin described had originally been sent to a
collector named H. C. Stevens in Oregon City, Oregon. When Berlin
sent copies of his correspondence to the Davenport Academy, Gass
was warned and advised to get the specimens back. Accordingly, he
wrote the Oregon collector on 30 January 1886: "I learned by letters . . . that the Indian pipe I exchanged with you some years ago is
not authentical and very doubtful just as you wrote to me when you
received it. I am very sorry I did not believe you and that I was so
badly mistaken. I got the whole lot sent to you from the same party
and now I am afraid there could be some more doubtful articles
among them and of course I never would give to any body a doubtful relic by my will and knowledge."[12] Gass continued the letter by
saying that he was sending Stevens's relics back to him by that
day's mail and was enclosing a postal money order to have his relics
returned. Stevens promptly replied that the specimens were no
longer his but belonged to Berlin. He added in his letter the comment: "I am sorry to say that not only the pipe, but the pipes, and
each and every other article received from you, were the basest kind
of frauds. Now it seems to me that a man of your reputation would
hardly be so easily imposed upon by such worthless trash."[13]

The remarks by Gass, including the phrase *not authentical and
very doubtful,* seem weak when confronted by Stevens's reply that
everything was the basest kind of fraud. We wonder, as Stevens and
others did, how Gass could be so easily fooled; this seems so unlikely that it appears Gass was not fooled but deliberately made up
phony relics for his trades. The letter that Gass sent to Oregon is
suspicious because it was composed at the Academy in broken English, instead of being an English translation of German. The Academy kept a reference copy in an attempt to get the frauds back
under cover.

Reverend Gass had moved to a new pulpit in Postville in 1883 and had explored various mounds in Allamakee and adjacent counties in northern Iowa. He was mentioned in the *Proceedings* from time to time as donating a few specimens or sending a note about his activities. News of the Gass-Stevens relic trading had been intimated by Peet as early as November 1885, and Putnam was furious when the correspondence was actually published in the *American Antiquarian* the following March of 1886. Another defense was needed, and Putnam set to work manufacturing one for publication.

In a letter dated 20 April 1886, Putnam wrote to the editor, Stephen Peet, that the defense of his activities in relic trading rested upon the clergyman's inability to express himself in English. Letters sent out under the signature of Gass had actually been dictated by him in German to his students, who in turn composed them in English. Gass had not thoroughly read the letters before they were mailed. Under such circumstances, mistakes were likely to occur. Since Gass did not write English, his defense would be translated at the Davenport Academy and forwarded to the *American Antiquarian* for publication as a rejoinder to the editorial and the Berlin correspondence.[14]

Peet replied that he would only publish the Gass defense if it were sent to him directly by the clergyman himself. If it was in German, the editor said he would have it translated for publication. His reluctance to publish a secondhand account received from the Academy stemmed from information he had received that an account was being manufactured by Putnam. "Mr. Gass has a right to be heard," he wrote, "but he will be heard in his own name and not through a lawyer who is seeking to catch me and make me trouble."[15] (Putnam was seeking to intimidate Peet with threats of libel, a matter that comes up again.) No rebuttal was ever published in the *American Antiquarian* because the editor suspected collusion between Putnam, Pratt, and Gass.

With that journal closed to him, Putnam turned to *Science* and published in May 1866 a lengthy rejoinder to the charges made by Berlin. Putnam wrote the introduction with legal skill. The items traded by Gass were "alleged fraudulent mound-relics." It is "plainly intimated that these disclosures tended to place all that gentleman's discoveries under the ban of suspicion." However, the publication of these letters was made without communicating with the Davenport Academy or "affording Mr. Gass an opportunity for explanation." This introduction was followed by a lengthy communication written to him by Gass, the translation of which was certified as correct by two prominent German-speaking citizens of Davenport.[16]

In this narrative in *Science*, Gass explained that the trading was not done on his own account but rather on behalf of the Academy. The curator, Mr. Pratt, authorized him to undertake the exchange, and accordingly he sent off a box of "primitive" implements originally received from Pastor Mutschman of Missouri. He originally gave no credit to Stevens's complaints because he felt they were made as an excuse to give little or nothing in exchange:

> As to who has written my letters for me, I cannot now say positively. Mrs. Gass says it was certainly done by one of my pupils, and I believe she is right. A letter in German, written by myself, would surely have sounded quite differently. These unfortunate letters have, however, been sent in my name, and with my name, and I must now abide the consequences, come what will. I can scarcely understand even (supposing that Mr. Berlin's copy of my letter is correct), how the incorrect statement that the Academy had bought such pipes, and paid such high prices for them, could have occurred unobserved. The boy who wrote the letter for me must have misunderstood me, and from my ignorance of the English language I overlooked this error.[17]

There were other equivocations. The clergyman wrote in his own defense that he was not sure that Stevens's claims were correct, for he had been unable to study the relics and determine if they were actually the ones that had been sent. Similarly, he had no way of knowing if Berlin had published an unaltered copy of his original letter. He concluded his statement by saying "That the intention or the thought of having any thing to do with doubtful relics, or of deceiving any one with them, was far from my mind, will to you, scarcely require any special assurance from me."[18] As a final comment on the line of defense, Putnam's opening remarks emphasized the clergyman's integrity of character. He then went on to state that this same moral test should be applied to the accusers. In a sense it was an unanswered question, for could those who made the charges about Gass provide as unblemished a record of their own activities? The reader of the defense was not told the answer, but the seeds of doubt had been planted.

In this *Science* article, Putnam had performed brilliantly. He viewed the scientific readers as an expanded type of jury, and he blunted the attack on Gass by raising a typical legalistic defense— *reasonable doubt.* The motives and the integrity of the accusers were suspect. It was not proven that the relics sent by Gass were the ones Stevens received and described. It was not proven that the letter was published accurately by Berlin. It could be firmly stated

that the letter was not even written by Gass and that he would not
have written such a letter. The whole affair was blown out of proportion and had simply been a customary exchange of relics between
the museum of the Academy and a private individual. Although the
collection obtained from a Missouri clergyman *allegedly* contained
fraudulent relics, the matter was not established, and in the last
analysis no one really knew more than that the collection contained
"primitive" objects that might or might not be genuine antiquities.
He successfully established his case for reasonable doubt concerning the charges, and those who wished to believe in the authenticity
of the slate tablets and elephant pipes could do so knowing that the
relic exchanges were not relevant to the Cook Farm excavations
and other research conducted by the clergyman.[19]

However, it is possible to look behind the surface of the defense
and examine some curious inconsistencies, about which no reader
of the *Science* article would have known. From unpublished correspondence, it is clear that the explanation resulted from collusion
between the curator of the Academy, the lawyer, and the clergyman. A letter from Gass dated 13 April 1886 admits as much. In
this communication—addressed from Postville and sent to the curator, Pratt—Reverend Gass: (1) acknowledged receipt of his own defense statement from the Academy; (2) said, "I have in general left
everything as it was" and only made minor changes; (3) added the
comment, "In case you find it desirable to make any changes you
may do so with entire freedom;" and (4) agreed to recopy the letter
in order to hide alterations. He wrote, "Should it be necessary to
copy the letter again, I will be ready at any time, but before Easter it
would not be possible."[20]

There is nothing wrong with having a manuscript reviewed before publication—quite the contrary, it is always desirable. The
problem, however, is determining Putnam's and Pratt's influence in
the defense allegedly written by Gass himself. It appears to be certain that most of it was actually composed for him.

The manufactured defense hid certain facts, to put a better face
on the affair. Gass admitted dictating letters that were unread before mailing, a matter that suggests a considerable traffic in relic
trading. It seems equally clear that this was not carried out for the
benefit of the Davenport Academy, regardless of what was later said
about it. Instead, it seems to have been for the benefit of Gass himself, a process of trading off phony relics for what he hoped were
genuine ones, to upgrade his collection. For example, he wrote
Stevens that he was mailing back the Oregon collection from Post-

ville, an impossible situation if the specimens were part of the Academy accessions. There is in fact no record in the museum today of any collection from Stevens being received.[21]

But on the surface of things, the controversy was still well in hand. *Reasonable doubt* had been cast upon the discussions of Henshaw, Foreman, and the complaints made by Berlin and Peet. Yet at the same time, a new challenge to the specimens appeared.

8

TIFFANY'S ORDEAL

Charles Putnam repeatedly elaborated the argument in print
that no member of the Academy doubted either the good faith of the
discoverers or the genuineness of the unique specimens. A. S. Tiffany's letter to the Bureau of Ethnology destroyed this argument
when excerpts were published in *Science* by Cyrus Thomas.[1] To
Putnam, it was obvious that a major effort needed to be made to
discredit Tiffany's testimony. He knew that several members were
talking about the tablets and pipes as frauds. If an example were
made of Tiffany, it would silence the objections and draw the whole
Academy behind Gass and the specimens in the midst of the controversy. Having decided upon a course of action, Charles Putnam
set up a committee to investigate Tiffany's conduct—handpicked
men who would humiliate Tiffany and vote to expel him from the
membership rolls.

The crucial role of Tiffany's letter in the controversy has been
described in my account of the exchange between Cyrus Thomas
and Putnam in the pages of *Science* in late 1885 and early 1886 (see
chapter 6).[2] The real letter itself never appeared—only short excerpts. Putnam challenged Thomas to publish it *verbatim ac litera-
tim* (by exact wording and spelling), saying that such publication
would destroy Tiffany's value as an authority and subject Thomas
himself to censure for relying on such sources of information.[3] The
letter of 27 October 1882 survives in copy and shows discrepancies
on both sides of the exchange. With its misspellings and lack of
punctuation, it reads in part:

Those shale tablets I have the utmost confidence that they are genuine I examined the situation when they ware first obtained The limestone tablet I am certain is a fraud   Mr Gass assisted in diging it out by Mr Harison and Mr John Hume   Mr Hume informs me that there was a wall of small bowlders around the tablet on the tablet there was some arrow points a quartz crystal and a unio shell filled with red paint the whole being covered with a rough lime stone slab the space betwene it and tabled not filled with earth and the paint bright and clean It is only nessisary to say the Mr Harison is a stone cutter

In regard to the eliphant pipes would say that the first pipe has no no history it is made of a coal measure sand rock which is very soft and friable it is saturated with grease which gives it the appearance of hardness and age   the one which Mr Gass dug from a mound is of the same material also saturated with grease it has the same finger marks as the first one and Mr Gass could be deceived with that plant as he was with the tablet Mr Gass is honest but he is not sharp. . . . I am loosing confidence in scientific authority and believe little except what I can verify with my own sences I am not working with out Academy nor doo I ever expect to[4]

The descriptions of Gass as honest but not sharp and Harrison as a stonecutter were bound to raise a threat of slander in the heated atmosphere. At the time of the hearing, Harrison was a pharmacist, but he seems to have been employed as a stonecutter at an earlier time, according to unpublished testimony by Tiffany and Dr. Lindley, which was not refuted. Putnam felt that the illiterate aspects of the letter weighed against its credibility. Thomas, on the other hand, relied on it as a knowledgeable local source. At the time it was written, Tiffany was feuding with the Academy, but he later participated in some of its affairs. Taken by itself, it had no value; but when added to growing evidence, it was devastating.

A special committee was appointed late in 1885 to investigate Tiffany's conduct in writing slanders about Academy members to the Smithsonian. The committee was chaired by H. C. Fulton, and C. H. Preston, acting as recording secretary, kept the minutes of the hearing and received all of the documents. The five members had read Tiffany's letter and wished to learn if his two statements could be confirmed: (1) that the two elephant pipes were saturated with grease to give the appearance of antiquity, and (2) that the limestone tablet was a "plant" in the Cook Farm mound. They also wished to learn if some of the other stories in circulation, but not written down, could be substantiated. To find out the answers, they requested written statements from Tiffany, the curator Pratt, and the three excavators of the limestone tablet—Harrison, Hume, and Gass. It all sounded appropriate and straightforward. In contrast to the illiteracy of his 1882 letter, Tiffany's 1885 defense to the committee had been rewritten in polished prose by his lawyer. It was seven pages long and typewritten on legal-size paper. Copies were widely circulated.

The first written charges against Tiffany were for "impeaching the genuineness of very important relics" and putting into circulation grave charges against the honor of his associate members without first presenting his charges to the Academy.[5] Tiffany replied that he did not have *absolute proof* that the relics were not what was claimed for them. As to the matter that he had implicated fellow members, his defense raised a curious issue. The only foundation for such a charge was obtained from a private letter written to Professor Norris some years previously. When excerpts of the letter appeared in *Science,* Putnam wrote to Cyrus Thomas, demanding a copy of the letter, as Tiffany himself had not made a copy of the original. In correspondence, Cyrus Thomas replied that he would not give a copy to Putnam but was sending one to Tiffany to do with as he pleased.[6] Putnam demanded the letter from Tiffany, received it, and *then* circulated it to the committee and others as the primary basis of the Academy charges—very much a breach of good faith. In his own defense, Tiffany said: "When a private correspondence must needs be ransacked in order to obtain evidence that a certain statement has been made it is bad enough. But when after obtaining such things in that manner, the letter itself is hawked about for the express purpose of informing persons of its contents, it comes with very poor grace to seek to charge the responsibility of 'circulating' it upon the writer."[7]

Meanwhile, Charles Harrison had become vice president of the Academy and was slated to become its president at the end of the year when Putnam's term expired. Harrison was the "stonecutter," and he threatened to sue Tiffany for libel, based upon the copy of the letter that Putnam had circulated. This threat had an immediate bearing upon the committee's investigation. The lawyer who represented Tiffany at the Academy hearing advised him against discussing the frauds in any detail *unless* the threat of Harrison's libel suit was removed. Harrison refused. Consequently, in order to protect himself, Tiffany gave no more information to the committee. His defense was muffled.

William Pratt—a longtime member, former president, and cur-
rently the full-time curator—intimately knew the men, the specimens, and the affairs of the Academy. His report, handwritten and
four-and-one-half pages long, carried weight.[8] Although judicious in
his discussion, he reported that he could find no evidence to support
Tiffany's written statements about the specimens. He began his
statement with the comment, "I do not recall any charge of fraud in
reference to the elephant pipes or limestone tablet being made to
the Academy, nor any particular conversation with Mr. Tiffany concerning doubts about them." He did recall that Tiffany had attempted to purchase the first elephant pipe from Reverend Gass for
five dollars after it had been broken. He was turned down and later
came back "much excited," told Gass that it was a fraud, and urged
him to return it to its former owner, the Louisa County farmer. The
implication of this story was that Tiffany might have made up the
story about the pipe being a fraud in order to purchase it for himself
from either the clergyman or its former owner.

Pratt continued by asserting that he had never detected a smell
of linseed oil or other grease on either of the elephant pipes. To the
best of his knowledge, no visitor to the museum nor any Academy
member had ever reported smelling oil on the pipes. The man who
accidentally broke the elephant pipe was Dr. R. D. Myers, and he
examined the inside surfaces very carefully and stated there was no
evidence of oil or grease on that pipe. Two of the pipes in the display
case did smell of linseed oil or putty, and he thought it possible that
someone hearing about it had mistakenly thought that it referred to
the elephant pipes.

Another story circulating among members of the Academy at
the time concerned the quartz crystal found on top of the limestone
tablet. Tiffany, in conversation, claimed it was from his own collection of minerals and had mysteriously reappeared in the excavation. Although the transcript of the committee hearings does not
relate the story of the crystal, Pratt referred to the matter in order to
suggest that Tiffany made it up to slander the Academy. Pratt stated
that the first he ever heard of the quartz-crystal story was in his
conversation of 1885 with the chairman of the investigating committee. No remarks were ever made seven years earlier when the
crystal was found with the tablet, and more tellingly, Pratt added,
Tiffany had not referred to the crystal in his 1882 letter to the
Smithsonian. His final testimony stated that it hardly seemed possible that anyone could have made a four-foot excavation into the
mound and built an altar of limestone without being observed, be-

cause the mound was in a very public place, just a few rods, a total
distance of some fifty to sixty feet, from the road to Smith's
(Schmidt's) limestone quarry.[9] Furthermore, there was no trace of
disturbance in the sod on top of the mound when the excavation
began. The committee put considerable weight upon the evidence
presented by the respected curator.

Charles Harrison's report to the committee was a brief two
pages, for he said he had published another report on the excavation of the limestone tablet.[10] His remarks were addressed to the
conduct of Tiffany. He reported that he had never heard any accusa-
tion or suggestion of fraud except for the stories that could be traced
to Tiffany. He added statements to the effect that he had talked with
Tiffany many times about different matters, but he had never been
questioned about the discovery of the limestone tablet and had
never been asked for fuller details. This line of testimony from the
vice president also carried conviction, for it authenticated the relics
and lay the blame solely on one dissident member.

It was beginning to look like a cut-and-dried matter for the committee to decide: even the defendant could not guarantee that the
relics were fakes, and all the testimony from the vice president and
the curator supported their authenticity. However, unexpected testimony was given by a member who was not a participant in the
excavation and whose information had not been sought by the committee. The self-appointed witness was a local physician, Dr.
Clarence Lindley. Dr. Lindley's difficulties with the Academy leadership had first occurred a year or so earlier, and they now broke into
the open when he began his personal defense of Tiffany.

In the Academy rooms at 3 p.m. on 4 March 1886, the committee
of investigation met to hear Dr. Lindley's testimony at a closed
meeting. The minutes state that President Putnam also attended.[11]
Dr. Lindley had been advised to avoid remarks that would bring a
libel suit against him for damages. Consequently, he denied any
knowledge about the affair, claimed he was misunderstood, and
then gave his testimony in the form of rhetorical questions. Who, he
mused, might know the answers?

1. Did the friends and members of D.A.N.S. [Davenport Academy of Natural Sciences] ever perpetrate an archaeological
   plant on A. S. Tiffany?
2. Did Chas. Harrison ever boast that he could make a 3000
   year old arrow in 5 minutes?
3. Have stone and marble cutters ever made tablets of hieroglyphics and passed them off for genuine relics of antiquity?

4. Have any of the members of the D.A.N.S. ever attended a
   meeting of the A.A.A.S. [American Association for the Advancement of Science] and there referred to Mr. Tiffany in a
   disrespectful way as a man unworthy of attention, as a
   crank?
5. Did the Rev. Mr. Gass ever see any fraudulent curved-base
   pipe?
6. Did the Rev. Mr. Blumer [Gass's brother-in-law] ever have a
   knowingly, fraudulent curved-base elephant pipe in his possession?

   Being asked as to his knowledge as to any of these questions, he refused to answer at this time.
   Being asked as to a statement that Mr. Graham's tools had
been used in making the l.s. [limestone] tablet, [he] refused to
explain at present.[12]

The questions were circumlocutions forced by legal threats
from Putnam and Harrison. John Graham was the janitor of the
Academy. The point of Dr. Lindley's testimony behind closed doors
was to show the committee that he and others knew the answers to
the unfortunate questions. Tiffany was not alone in raising doubts
about some of the relics. The clear hint given was that if Tiffany had
done a little name-calling, others had made public remarks in return. The matter should be dropped, for the public answers to the
questions would result in a scandal.

Before Dr. Lindley had left his questions ringing in the ears of
the committee, another man had spoken—the brother of the vice
president, John Harrison. At Putnam's request, the brother made
the statement that both Harrisons would resign if Tiffany continued
as a member.[13] This put the committee on notice that one side or the
other would leave the group either voluntarily or involuntarily.
Since Charles Harrison was prominent in Academy affairs, his absence would be a loss. Moreover, it would indeed look strange to the
world if a principal discoverer of the limestone tablet disavowed all
further connection with the Academy.

The committee had been pressured. At a subsequent public
meeting, Lindley hotly declared,

The investigation began. One question was asked him. "Did you
write any such letters?" He confessed to this one, and that
stopped the investigation. No more was gone through with. The
committee then disbanded to sign a paper that was to expel Mr.
Tiffany, and not reprimand him as was represented to
him . . . The committee told Mr. Tiffany he was not going to be

> expelled. [They] told the friends and relatives of Mr. Tiffany that
> he was not going to be expelled. Mr. Tiffany goes away. He leaves
> for the far west. In his absence after telling him he was not going
> to be expelled, what did the members of this institution do?[14]

Lindley's rhetorical question was asked at the public meeting that followed the conclusion of the closed sessions by the investigating committee. This committee had passed a motion to recommend expelling Tiffany, without the alternative of censure. The threat made by the two Harrisons to resign had had its desired effect. Under the rules, the Academy's general meeting was left without the option of chiding Tiffany while allowing him to continue as a member, despite verbal promises to the contrary. Lindley's testimony had been of no help and had probably made matters worse. Yet the committee felt satisfied that it had done a good job, primarily because of the statement prepared by Pratt that such stories as the grease-soaked elephant pipes and the discovery of Tiffany's quartz crystal on top of the limestone tablet were just that—stories, with no foundation in fact.[15]

9

THE PUBLIC EXPULSION
OF TIFFANY

The stout defense of A. S. Tiffany by Cyrus Thomas published in *Science* in late February made no impression whatever on the Davenport Academy.[1] It is possible the members read only Putnam's side of the issue. In March 1886 the committee reported to a meeting of twenty-eight members that A. S. Tiffany should be expelled from membership. It was a hard decision to reach because he had been a founder of the Academy nearly twenty years earlier. But those who may have doubted that the Putnam forces had the votes to carry off the expulsion were soon taught a lesson.

Although there was some routine business, the purpose of this meeting was known to be a ratification of the findings and conclusions of the special committee. Its chairman, H. C. Fulton, read the report, and the motion was made. The following record is from the original handwritten copy of the minutes written by the secretary, Dr. Jennie McCowen, one of the first women to be a practicing physician in Iowa. I have added some punctuation, deleted as indicated in the text, and added an occasional connecting word. The transcript vividly conveys the heat of the discussion over the Davenport controversy. The second vice president, J. B. Phelps, presided because the first vice president, Charles Harrison, was a principal in the contention.[2]

> *Dr. Lindley* objected to the resolution. He thought the Academy could not afford to expel one of its "chartered" members. Mr. Tiffany had been an active and valuable member, and had on

two different occasions saved the life of the Academy when it was gasping for breath. The beginning of the library was due to him. Mr. Tiffany had agreed to tell all he knew if criminal charges were not brought against him. He did not bring his charges before the Academy because past communications had been smothered. He had good reasons for making the charges he did. He knew frauds had been committed. He knew these tablets were frauds. Mr. Harrison had openly boasted of being able to make 3,000 year old arrow heads in five minutes—

Mr. Harrison rose to a point of order.

Dr. Lindley: "O, well, if you don't want the light let in on you, all right."

Chairman Phelps: It is hardly necessary for Dr. Lindley to act as advocate for Mr. Tiffany. This matter has been thoroughly considered by the Committee and it is not necessary perhaps to debate it further.

Objections were made by various members to cutting off debate.

Mr. Fulton called attention to the fact that Mr. Harrison's point of order was that Dr. Lindley was wandering from the point and indulging in personalities not connected with the subject under discussion and that the ruling of the Chair was meant to be in the same direction. No one objected to the fullest and freest debate of the questions properly before us.

The Chair so ruled.

On motion of Mr. Putnam, it was unanimously voted to allow Dr. Lindley to proceed.

Dr. Lindley said he was not here as an advocate for Mr. Tiffany, but thought he was not having fair treatment. Some of the most respected citizens of this place believe Mr. Tiffany to be an ill-used old gentleman. Both officers and members have tried in every way to belittle him. Members have in the Association for the Advancement of Science called him an "old crank" and not entitled to any consideration. He would ask, had Mr. Tiffany any reasons for the course he pursued. He (Dr. Lindley) thought he had. Could he be expected to bring any charges in the Academy when his former communications had been carefully smothered? He thought not. As for this Committee, it was one-sided and did not want to reach the facts in the case. He (Dr. Lindley) was called before that Committee. He had 45 questions which would have thrown some light on this subject but they refused to hear them. Mr. Tiffany knew frauds had been committed but when threatened with a suit for libel if he told what he knew, of course he refused to do it. Mr. Tiffany is not alone in this. Some of the most respected members of this Academy believe these tablets to be a fraud. Mr. Tiffany *knew* curved-base pipes had been made in the Academy; that Mr. Harrison had made fraudulent tablets and passed them off as genuine.

The Academy is yearly losing in membership and we will take a wrong step and damage ourselves if we expel this old gentleman especially when he is not present to defend himself. This Academy owes an apology to Mr. Tiffany instead of a vote of expulsion.

Mr. Pilsbury called attention to the fact that Mr. Tiffany had had ample opportunity to make any defense he chose before the Committee.

On motion of Mr. Putnam it was unanimously voted to allow Dr. Lindley to read his 45 questions.

After some hesitation, *Dr. Lindley* said they were pertinent to the subject—but he thought he would not read them. It did not seem to be the proper time. He wished another Committee appointed who would be just and honest and would take into consideration all the facts in the case which ought to be investigated. This has got to be done sooner or later and when this Committee is appointed he would lay his questions before them.

Dr. Hazen said he did not rise as a champion of Mr. Tiffany nor of his conduct. Five members of this Academy, honorable men, chief members of the Academy, had carefully and thoroughly considered the question. Undoubtedly, their conclusions were sound and entitled to credence. Yet he personally had a good deal of sympathy for Mr. Tiffany. He had been a prominent member ever since the beginning. He had by personal solicitation collected from the citizens the first $300 which commenced our library, and he had been active in many ways in building up the Academy. He may be peculiar in many ways, eccentric. He may have been honest in his beliefs in regard to this matter—but mistaken. We think he *was* mistaken.

The Committee have not examined into the genuineness of the tablets but that is involved and ought to be considered. We ought to think well before tossing out an old man who has done so much. It ought to be very plain why we take such a step. I have a good deal of sympathy for Mr. Tiffany; there are many genuine, good things about him.

I think this resolution for expulsion is going to pass and I must say I think it ought to pass, but I don't think the resolution is plain enough. It ought to state more clearly that Mr. Tiffany's conduct is the point at issue and not the genuineness of the tablets or his doubting their genuineness.

The genuineness of the tablets is yet an open question, and we should always be ready to give a hearing to any honest argument or any competent testimony. All that we can claim is that the find was a genuine find made in good faith by the members of this Academy engaged in the search. Further than that we cannot say. . . .

Mr. Holmes said he had had little previous knowledge of this affair and was greatly surprised at what he had heard here this evening. It seemed from what had been said, that Mr. Tiffany being a member of the Academy was using his position from within to furnish the enemies of the institution with ammunition for its destruction. It seems he is making open statements to the world derogatory to its character and standing, is calling in question the integrity and honor of its members and then refuses to give the reasons for his belief or to bring forward the proof, which he says he has, in support of his statements. The defense attempted here for Mr. Tiffany is a charge against the good faith of the Committee and fresh charges against other members. If he thought this Academy so unjust, unfair and unscrupulous as we have heard this evening he should want to withdraw at once. He should not want to have anything to do with such a set of men.

Again, the right of the Academy to protect itself is challenged. He had not known much of this matter before, but it needed no other education than he had received on this occasion to make it clear that from the evidence offered here this evening the issue is a square one and one which must be promptly met.

Dr. Parry said no one was more reluctant than he take measures against Mr. Tiffany. He had been on friendly terms with him for many years and had respect for what was true in the man. He was very loath to take any action which might seem hasty and as Mr. Tiffany was not present to speak for himself, he moved that action be postponed.

Mr. Kracke wished, if this motion prevailed, to add to it that Mr. Tiffany be notified to put in an appearance and defend himself.

Mr. Fulton called attention to the fact that this matter had *not* been hastily acted upon. It had been under consideration for *three months*. He had personally informed Mr. Tiffany that the report would be offered at this meeting. He had also notified Mr. Tiffany's attorney of the fact. The matter was well understood in all quarters.

Mr. Fulton regretted to the utmost that he had, after giving the most careful and thorough attention to this matter, found it his duty to sign the report as given by the Committee. There was no escaping the conclusion that in this case, heroic treatment was necessary and in his opinion now was the time. He was opposed to any postponement unless it could be shown wherein anything was to be gained by it.

Prof. Call hoped the motion would not prevail as it cast an imputation on the Committee.

Motion to postpone lost by unanimous vote. . . .

Mr. Thompson said that point had been very clearly kept in view throughout all this investigation and he thought it was clearly expressed in the findings of the Committee. Mr. Tiffany, his attorney, and his friends had continually tried to divert them from the main point, which was *Mr. Tiffany's* conduct. The argument offered that he should not be dealt with because he had once worked with the Academy and helped build it up was no argument at all, but rather an aggravation of his offense. The greater his activity in the past, the more reprehensible his conduct now.

Mr. Judy wished information in regard to the matter of expressing doubts of the genuineness of any relics first to the Academy; and asked if it was the sense of the members that, for example, he could not be allowed to write a private letter to a friend giving an adverse opinion of anything in the collection without first submitting such doubts to the Academy.

Prof. Call said that writing a letter, even if to a personal friend, who was to be an employee of a government Bureau, to be presented to the head of the Bureau and used in scientific circles to our prejudice was a very different affair from such a letter as contemplated in Mr. Judy's remarks.

Mr. Fulton thought the purport of his resolution was misapprehended but with the consent of his second he would strike out the wording objected to, which he accordingly did.

Mr. Judy withdrew his substitute, as with this change Mr. Fulton's resolution met his approval.

Dr. Hazen's substitute lost.

Prof. Call seconded the original resolution as amended.

The motion being put seemed carried by a large majority. Dr. Parry calling for the yeas and nays, the vote stood as follows: [Aye 25, No 2]. . . .

Dr. Preston called attention to the statements made by Dr. Lindley in his speech in defense of Mr. Tiffany and thought they demanded notice.

Dr. Hazen thought no attention ought to be paid to anything said in the heat of debate.

Dr. Preston said these things had been said not only here and now, but also at other times and to various and sundry persons. Dr. Lindley had openly called in question the honesty and integrity of our Curator and had charged fraud upon other members. He thought we could not afford to ignore such statements and ought not wait.

Dr. Lindley said he wanted a committee appointed but hoped it would be a just and honest one that would be fair in its action, and one authorized to consider the whole question at issue.

Dr. Lindley desired to have G. W. French on the Committee, and his name was willingly accepted by the mover.

There being some further desultory talk as to what had been said, *Mr. J. H. Harrison* protested against any further consideration of the subject. It had been referred to a Committee and the proper place now for these questions to come up was before this Committee.

10

SUPPRESSION OF LINDLEY'S EVIDENCE

Dr. Clarence Lindley met with the committee appointed to investigate his charges on Thursday afternoon, 22 May 1886, in a meeting room of the Academy. The session was closed to the general membership, and the committee heard lengthy and embittered testimony, charges and countercharges. Although not a trial by law, it had the form and even the air of a courtroom drama. Complete records were kept of the testimony and the proceedings. The committee was chaired by the second vice president, J. B. Phelps, who had presided over the expulsion of Tiffany. The membership did not have any specific evidence from Dr. Lindley about the frauds, only his unsupported word. A number of members now felt that a new committee would be more thorough and resolve the relic controversy one way or the other.[1]

The chairman, Phelps, was a supporter of the relics and sided with Putnam's efforts to root out the dissident members. Putnam strengthened Phelps's resolve to deal firmly with the matter and wrote him that "this miserable business should be disposed of at the earliest moment practicable." In another letter, he wrote that Lindley's accusations were of "minor importance."[2] The hearings were clearly partisan and run by the Putnam faction.

By prior arrangement, Dr. Lindley called the janitor of the Academy, John Graham, to the stand to testify before the committee. A reluctant witness, the janitor was subjected to a cross-examination by the physician.

Lindley: You have been janitor here several years?

Graham: Yes.

Question: [You] have not been talked to in regard to certain charges except today?

Reply: No.

Question: Did you get pieces of stone and make curved base pipes?

Reply: Yes.

Question: Where did you make them?

Reply: Made one at home. Elephant pipe. Nearly like one here at the Academy.

Question: Did you not do some of your work here?

Reply: No—except possibly to make hole larger for stem.

Question: Did you not block it out here?

Reply: No—may have broken off corners of a piece of stone here.

Question: What became of the pipe?

Reply: Had same at the Academy. Mr. Pratt and Mr. Bloomer [Rev. Adolph Blumer] saw it. I smoked it.

Question: What about other pipes you made?

Reply: Made four pipes altogether. Did not make any of them here. Might have made hole for stem larger here at the Academy.

Question: Do you remember the Bear pipe?

Reply: Yes. Never finished it. Had one called Seal pipe—

Question: You remember about curved base pipes!

Reply: Yes, the elephant pipe. Mr. Pratt, Mr. Bloomer, Mr. Gass all saw it. Mr. Bloomer took it. Have not seen it since.

Question: Are any pipes here represented? (Shows cuts). Curved base pipes?

Reply: No. Might be slight curve near the end. The Elephant pipe was curved. Took the block of stone from here to make the Elephant pipe.

Question by Committee: Did you ever pass off any pipe or pipes you made as mound-builder relics?

Reply: No.

Question by Committee: Did you ever know of any such relics being passed off as genuine?

Reply: No.[3]

Three drawings pinned to the handwritten transcript portray platform-effigy pipes—a seal, a human foot, and a human head—and the handwritten caption on each says, "Pipe made by Jn. Graham." The elephant pipe is not represented among the drawings. These seem to be the "cuts" shown by Lindley during his testimony (figure 10.1).

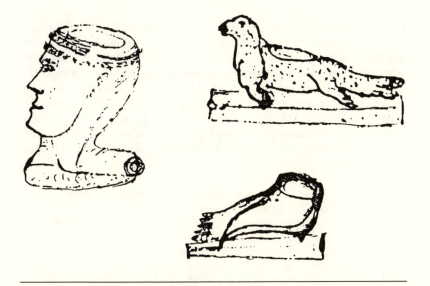

10.1 Effigy pipes made by the janitor, John Graham. These three sketches were appended to the testimony at the hearing; the elephant pipe sketch is missing. (Putnam Museum)

Graham, as a witness, clearly hedged, and his equivocation is important when seeking to trace the history of the elephant pipe found by Blumer in the Louisa County mound. Despite Graham's statement to the committee that he had no knowledge of fraudulent relics, he had made an elephant like the *one* in the Academy collection. But in 1880 there were *two* in the collection. The copy was last seen in the hands of Reverend Blumer, in company with his brother-in-law, Gass. I strongly suspect that John Graham's elephant, partially made in the basement, is the specimen that turned up in the excavation. Lindley was unable to confirm it during his questioning, and in looking at the janitor's testimony, it appears that Phelps cut off the discussion by asking questions for the committee. Graham was under pressure, for if he admitted that the second elephant was a homemade fraud, both he and his wife, Rachel, would lose their Academy jobs.

Lindley himself presented a sworn, notarized statement to the committee. In it he states "that between the first day of January 1880 and the first day of January 1885 I have seen curved base pipes in the process of manufacture in the building owned and occu-

pied by the Davenport Academy of Science. And further, affiant
saith not." January 1880 fits with the second elephant-pipe discovery later in the same year. Lindley, the affiant (a legal term for one
who makes an affidavit), was cautious and did not give names in the
document.[4] He did mention some in his verbal testimony, however.

As a practicing physician, Dr. Lindley seems to have suspected
that all was not well with the curator, Pratt. He consequently began
a curious line of questioning about Pratt's emotional stability, which
his reluctant witnesses, the janitor and the janitor's wife, did their
best to evade.

> *Lindley:* Have you ever seen Mr. Pratt in this institution?
> *Graham:* Yes, often—
> *Question:* Have you seen Mr. Pratt in a passion, throw books
> around, etc.?
> *Reply:* Yes, we all do that at times.
> *Question:* Has he used profane language often?
> *Reply:* No, no often. Might have said d—n it, or something
> like that—
> *Question:* Does he get excited, throw books and papers!
> *Reply:* Not often. Possibly may have thrown books or papers
> off the table. Has some passions. Did not always control him-
> self—
> *Question:* Has he slammed doors etc. when he lost his tem-
> per?
> *Reply:* Can't recollect [to] mind. Slams doors sometimes.
> Bolt was out once and [he] broke bolt or lock.
> *Question:* Did he lose his temper?
> *Reply:* Yes, was often tried. I often tried his temper. Could
> see he was irritated sometimes.[5]

Later in the transcript, Dr. Lindley attempted to get further information from the janitor's wife, Rachel Graham.

> *Lindley:* You are doorkeeper here?
> *Rachel Graham:* Yes. . . .
> *Question:* Have [you] seen Mr. Pratt about the Academy,
> have you seen him excited and throw things?
> *Reply:* Yes—a paper or something like that—
> *Question:* Did you see him in temper so as to be afraid of
> him?
> *Reply:* No.[6]

The doctor stopped this line of questioning when Rachel Graham
replied negatively. She had not been afraid, and so Pratt's emotional

stability was upheld. The curator, however, did seem to have an extraordinarily high temper for a man in his sixties.

According to Pratt's later complaints about this testimony, Lindley had "endeavored to prove by Graham and Rachel that I was in the habit of 'frequently, *very* frequently' getting into an ungovernable rage, grossly profane, slamming doors and throwing things around and wrecking things generally: so absolutely losing all control of myself as to be 'not responsible for my actions.' His witnesses disclaimed knowledge of any such conduct on my part. Lindley said '*I have seen it dozens and dozens of times.*'" Pratt related this incident, along with others, to show that Lindley was a liar.[7]

The Grahams' testimony made the curator look foolish and raised damaging questions about relic manufacture in the Academy itself. What had happened to the homemade pipes? In response, Harrison, Pratt, Putnam, and others counterattacked. They attempted to show Phelps and his committee that Dr. Lindley was dishonest, untrustworthy, and a crank. They attacked his character to prove that the physician was an unreliable witness and that responsible men should have a *reasonable doubt* about his testimony. It was a typical courtroom maneuver. There is a great deal of manuscript testimony about these charges, and a summary of some parts of it becomes relevant when evaluating the Academy as a scientific organization.

It comes as a surprise to learn that Dr. Lindley had been practicing medicine in the Academy itself. According to Lindley, "the trustees requested me to practice here." Charles Harrison finally ordered the doorkeeper, Rachel Graham, to inform Lindley's patients that he did not have an office in the Academy. This had angered the doctor, who maintained that Mrs. Putnam was behind the removal because she did not like his patients: "Mrs. Putnam said they were not high toned enough to come here."[8] While a resident of the building, the physician had had ample opportunity to observe the activities of both the janitor and the curator.

Pratt wrote a formal statement to the committee that Dr. Lindley was the only member of the Academy he knew who might be making fraudulent relics. Pratt said he had no doubts about any of the archeological specimens in the Academy itself. There was, however, an exception: "C. T. Lindley has rechipped broken flint implements, whether passed off by him as entirely original Indian work or not, I do not know; and, I have not examined the specimens in his collection and do not know as to the genuineness or history of them."[9] Lindley never denied that he chipped flint.

In the early years, the Academy provided storage space for the private collections of its members. Today it is a violation of ethical practices for archaeologists to own artifacts; specimens must become part of established, publicly owned collections to document their research. The Davenport Academy was a scientific organization, but the archaeological research was relic hunting carried out by amateurs, and the rules were very lax. Members pillaged sites; sometimes kept their finds; and bought, sold, and traded to improve their collections. This, of course, had brought Reverend Gass into difficulties, when it was learned that he was mailing frauds to other collectors.

Dr. Lindley did not give most of his specimens to the Academy but built up a large, apparently valuable private collection of artifacts. He insisted that the Academy continue to provide the storage service for its members. This again brought him into conflict with Mrs. Putnam, who had complained about his patients visiting the Academy. Mrs. Putnam was quoted as saying somewhat publicly, "When my husband gets to be president your collection will have to come out." In January 1886, Pratt hired a local firm to haul Lindley's collection away, to be redeemed upon payment of cartage and storage. Pratt, a compulsive saver, preserved the receipt in the official papers.[10]

Several years after the affair was closed, Pratt was still writing memos about the disreputable conduct of Tiffany and Lindley. One of these, dating from 1889, is a rather lengthy manuscript proving that Lindley's collection was not destroyed in a fire in 1887 and therefore he was not entitled to receive three thousand dollars in compensation. It had been stored in the State Orphan's Home at the time of the fire, and a state claim was filed for damages. The size of the claim Lindley made was not only large, it was a preposterous valuation for local antiquities at the time it was made.[11]

Lindley and his opponents wrangled over many other charges before the committee, and the independent members who attempted to evaluate the situation were confused by the obfuscations and personality conflicts that had little or nothing to do with the matter of the genuineness of the inscribed tablets and elephant pipes. In an attempt to bring the issues into clearer focus, the report of the committee summarized Dr. Lindley's charges in a statement that was subsequently published in the *Proceedings* of the Academy. Lindley had said:

1. That curved base pipes were made in the Academy;
2. That people about town know it;

3. That Mr. Pratt [the curator] knows all about it;
4. He (Lindley) not only knew that they were made, but had seen them made;
5. Mr. Tiffany had good reasons for his conduct, he knew the tablets were frauds, and that other frauds were committed;
6. He is not alone in this belief; it is shared by some of the most respected members of the Academy;
7. Mr. Harrison has made fraudulent tablets, and passed them off as genuine;
8. Mr. Pratt is dishonest in that if he should pack his (Lindley's) collection, he would drop out and leave behind the most valuable specimens;
9. The committee on Tiffany's conduct did not want to reach the facts in the case, and were neither just nor fair in their action;
10. There are "goings on" at the Academy which he is going to throw light upon. He is going to see that every scientist in Europe hears of these things, and every time they are smoothed over he is going to "boom it up again."[12]

There is also a mass of unpublished testimony in the files of the case. From a letter Putnam wrote at the outset of Lindley's hearing, it can be seen that the above charges were originally stated in a more colloquial fashion. One can compare, for example, the first statement made above with the manuscript: "First: Curved base pipes have been made in the Academy. If people in town knew how many, their eyes would be opened." The other charges also vary somewhat from manuscript to printed copy. The manuscript version contains an eleventh charge that "there is a plot or conspiracy to injure him," a not unreasonable complaint by Lindley, considering the activities of Putnam and his friends.[13]

What would be the conclusion drawn by the committee about this mass of claims and testimony? They reported that Lindley denied having accused Harrison of making fraudulent tablets. The committee then reported back to the Academy president *that none of the charges made by Dr. Lindley were sustained.*

This, of course, was a misrepresentation of the facts. The janitor's testimony established Dr. Lindley's charge that curved-base pipes had been worked on inside the Academy and also substantiated the fact that Gass, Blumer, and Pratt all knew about the manufacture of pipes. This testimony also demonstrated that the first committee had not been seeking information on the specimens and thus "did not want to reach the facts in the case." By its action, the second committee had avoided the facts with equal facility.

However, in defense of the committee's judgment, Lindley had been unable to prove that any of the manufactured specimens had been later placed in the Indian burial mounds. All he had been able to demonstrate was the harmless amusement of men who made copies of genuine relics for their own purposes—such as smoking. The janitor specifically denied any wrongdoing.

In May 1886, the committee of inquiry brought its resolution to the general Academy membership for a vote. It was resolved that Dr. Clarence Lindley should be expelled from the membership and his name struck from the roll. The reasons given were his unfounded charges, his hostility to the Davenport Academy, and his persistence in disturbing its peace and harmony. Among other findings, the committee concluded that retention of Dr. Lindley as a member would injure the standing of the Academy within the community. The physician refused to leave the room during the discussion and vote.

From the minutes, it appears that not one member defended Lindley. A few of the statements illustrate the outspoken debate. Professor Sheldon claimed, "You can see by the report which has been made that not one of the charges was sustained. Not a particle of truth was found. I have much confidence in the committee in following up each and every point. . . ." In a lengthy rejoinder, Lindley replied: "I do not know if I can make it as plain as I ought to; I know that Mr. Tiffany has made certain relics in the basement of the Academy and my speech had reference to the relics that the janitor made in the cellar. So far as saying Mr. Pratt was engaged in making such things, I never intimated anything of the kind. Nothing whatever."[14] William H. Holmes said in rebuttal:

> Dr. Lindley has taken a course that compels us in self-defense to expel him as a member and exclude him from further usefulness. . . . I believe him honest in the matter, though laboring under a great hallucination. . . . The action of Dr. Lindley threatens the life of the Academy. It certainly does. . . . We are called forgers, liars and perpetrators of iniquity, manufacturers of antique works. . . . When insinuations and denunciations of this sort are brought against us, I would acknowledge no private feelings whatever in the effort to free ourselves.

(Holmes, a nationally recognized archaeologist, was appointed honorary curator of pottery at the National Museum, Smithsonian

Institution, and was a research associate at the Bureau of Ethnology itself! When these remarks were made in May 1885, Holmes had published a lengthy, highly regarded study, "Ancient Pottery of the Mississippi Valley." It first appeared in the *Davenport Academy Proceedings,* 1884, and subsequently in the Fourth Annual Report of the U.S. Bureau of Ethnology in 1886. He used genuine specimens from the Academy collections in his publications. Unaware of the extent of the frauds, Holmes took a stand against Dr. Lindley to preserve the Academy as a research institution.)

Finally, Professor Sheldon summarized the feelings of the assembly when he moved to cut off debate. The previous speaker had suggested that the physician should have one more chance to defend himself from the charges. To this suggestion Sheldon replied:

> I should truly second that motion if Dr. Lindley has something new to offer. Something wherein he does not propose to make any charges against the Society. It is clear to me that Dr. Lindley should have no grounds for complaint. The Dr. has taken more time than all the rest together, and the last time, the time occupied was such that the chairman was unable to attend to unfinished business. Nothing more can be said further, and I move that the business of the evening he completed.[15]

The outcome of the debate over the committee report was a vote of thirty-six to none for expelling the physician and reestablishing peace and harmony.

11

SECRET INQUIRIES
AND LEGAL THREATS

The attacks in *Science* and the *American Antiquarian* were successfully blunted, and the two principal dissidents were removed to show the scientific world that the Academy membership backed the authenticity of the unique relics. With good reason, one could accept the interpretation that the ancient Mound Builders were a lost race from the Near East or Europe who had immigrated into the Midwest when the mastodon were still roaming the Mississippi valley.

After such a victory, one might expect Charles Putnam to rest from his labors. Yet he did not. He was firmly and totally committed to the enormous importance of the relics, and he was also convinced that the men who found them were honest. If these "undoubted facts" were true, the professional scientists might have ulterior motives for their attacks. For this reason, Charles Putnam decided to embark on a personal crusade to expose the villains who were conspiring against the Davenport Academy.

The theme of plotters who sought to destroy the Academy took strange forms, but the belief in a conspiracy was widespread among local members. The role of plotters came up in the debates over the Tiffany and Lindley resolutions. Any unexplained activity was thought to be part of the conspiracy. For example, there was a *geological fraud*. Someone had given the Academy some fossils of an unusual type, which turned out to be made from plaster of paris. There is a handwritten note from a former member—E. W. Claypole of Akron, Ohio—addressed to Pratt and dated from the height of the turmoil in February 1886. Claypole wrote,

> I am afraid you are right in regard to those pseudo-fossils and they were a trap laid by somebody for the Academy. I wish however you would set the whole thing at rest for ever by analysing the material which I am confident you will find to be Plaster of Paris. . . . I feel very glad you have never committed yourselves to it in any way for it would have hurt you much in the controversy about the elephant pipes.[1]

Given this set of mind, one can understand the confusion and resentment that existed in Davenport. Putnam sincerely believed that the Smithsonian Institution was engaged in a conspiracy to destroy the Academy by slander and innuendo. He believed that he could expose the conspiracy through libel suits, which would expose the principal plotters. His mind made up about the danger, Putnam began to hire agents to investigate anyone who published doubts about the genuineness of the Davenport tablets.

In an envelope preserved with the Tiffany file at the museum, there is a note postmarked January 1886, Washington, D.C. It is anonymous and possesses neither an address nor a salutation: "Are you aware that Powell has bought Peet up with a salary? That is the "true inwardness" of his "change of heart"—Let your Congressman or some friend in Washington see into it, and keep this letter a secret—burn it, in fact. A Friend of Justice."[2] The handwriting does not match any in the collection of correspondence, but the quotation marks suggest it was a reply to a previous query. In any event, confidential inquiries were to follow.

With growing suspicion, Putnam decided it was now necessary to investigate Reverend Stephen Peet of the *American Antiquarian* to find out if the latter's doubts about the unique relics were due to a financial link between him and the Bureau of Ethnology. It will be remembered that Peet had originally editorialized against the methods used by Henry Henshaw in the first published attempt to discredit the pipes and tablets. In January 1886, Peet published his first doubts about the relics and followed this with the publication of the Berlin correspondence about Reverend Gass's selling and trading of fraudulent specimens. At about the same time, Peet agreed to work as an archaeological assistant for the Bureau of Ethnology, investigating mounds in Wisconsin, where he lived. Peet is listed among the field-workers in the *Annual Report* from the Bureau of

Ethnology. Putnam's informer in Washington had correct information about the salary offer, which was accepted. Putnam suspected collusion. He sent off two letters to an attorney, William Jones, who lived in Clinton, Wisconsin. In almost illegible handwriting, Jones finally replied:

> Mr. Peet is highly resp'ct'd in this community. My personal estimate of him is that he is a gentleman of integrity & high character.
>
> I greatly regret the intelligence you communicate. I hope it may turn out that the exact facts do not warrant your indictment of him.
>
> As to his goods, moneys, rentals. If he has of these any thing where-with-al to satisfy an execution, I know nothing thereof, but my belief is that such an instrument would have to be returned "De bonis non."
>
> As to the "Magazine," you probably are yourself aware that his connection therewith commits in no wise to a leviable interest.
>
> As to my participating with you in a prosecution of the "Case." My relations with him are such that must be excused. . . . "[3]

From this letter, Putnam learned that Reverend Peet was well regarded locally and was safe from a libel suit because he had no money to pay damages. This did not end the matter, however, for Putnam decided upon a campaign of more direct harassment against the clergyman. Reverend Peet described it in a letter addressed to Putnam himself and dated 27 April 1886: "Your various communications have been received. I have felt under no particular obligations to answer them. In the first place, you seem to have undertaken to get at me through the courts, and have even come to members of my own congregation to make me trouble.

Second, you threaten to publish all the correspondence, private and personal, as well as that which is of public interest. . . . "[4]

This letter from Peet to Putnam reveals depressing aspects of the attorney's personality. He had evidently gone beyond what must have been the two strongly worded inquiries to Jones in Clinton, Wisconsin. Peet was vulnerable. In this modern day of scholarly journals, it is sometimes difficult to remember the difficulty such ventures had in this country a century ago. Peet ran his journal single-handedly and supported himself by preaching. By going to members of Peet's congregation, Putnam was deliberately cutting into his sole source of economic support. There may have been some dissatisfaction with Peet among local members because of the amount of time Peet required to work on his journal: editing, writing, soliciting articles, and acting as circulation manager as well. This must have detracted from the performance of his pastoral duties. Putnam saw a chance to get at Peet effectively through the congregation, and indeed Peet moved both himself and the *American Antiquarian* to Mendon, Illinois, in the fall of 1887. Since that town in 1870 had a population of about five hundred, we may imagine that the ministerial duties were neither well recompensed nor prestigious.

The threat to publish Peet's "private and personal" correspondence is a puzzle, since the only communications in the file are routine letters between Peet, Putnam, and Pratt—letters primarily concerned with Peet's refusal to publish Gass's defense against charges that he was selling or trading fraudulent artifacts. As has been previously explained, Peet correctly deduced that there was collusion in the preparation of the defense, for Gass himself admitted to Pratt that he had received the defense and would recopy it in his own handwriting. I don't know what is involved in the "personal" correspondence, since no trace of it appears in the files. It appears that Putnam purchased or otherwise obtained letters that no longer survive, a matter having overtones of blackmail. Putnam did not make idle threats.

Although Peet rejected the authenticity of the inscribed tablets and considered that Reverend Gass had been a victim of a series of hoaxes, the editor of the *American Antiquarian* continued to accept the validity of the elephant pipes.[5] It would appear that the legal and economic pressures applied by Putnam were not aimed at forcing Peet to recant on his stand about the tablets, but were intended to drive the journal out of business and get revenge for publishing the awkward correspondence about Reverend Gass.

Questioning the genuineness of the tablets and the elephant pipes was a serious affair to Putnam. In an effort to find out about A. F. Berlin, to whom he attributed the basest motives for publishing the Gass-Stevens correspondence, Putnam wrote to the legal firm of R. E. Wright's Sons in Allentown, Pennsylvania. He found that the local lawyers were eager to do business. His letter of 12 March 1886 reached them on 15 March; their answer was postmarked the same day and was stamped received in Davenport on 17 March. Thus, five days after sending his inquiry, Putnam received the following reply:

Mr. A. F. Berlin is a young man whose only business has been that of salesman, though I believe he does have a collection of objects that indicate that his mind is affected with feeble aspirations towards thoughts "scientific."

He is respectable as the world goes but narrow minded, bigoted and with all the self-assurance that usually comes with ignorance.

He is a man of limited means however and owns no property that we know of.

There is nothing to prevent our being concerned against him in litigation.[6]

Stevens, who corresponded with Gass and complained to Berlin about receiving fraudulent relics, was another man in the "plot to attack the Academy," and Putnam thought that he should be investigated and confronted with legal harassment. Accordingly, he dispatched a letter to Oregon City, Oregon, addressed to a firm of attorneys. Sent 12 March 1886, the letter was answered almost immediately:

"Yours of the 12" inst. came to hand yesterday—It was in reference to one H. C. Stevens R. R. agt. & ck.—Yes, we know the man well. He is financially responsible. He has the reputation of being *ordinarily* truthful and honest—He has some real estate—and some money at interest, and is probably worth from $5,000 to $7,000 dollars—

If desired we could act with you in libel suit against him if you have a good case.[7]

Such correspondence shows the vicious turn the defense of the Davenport specimens had taken. In 1886 A. F. Berlin wrote in the *American Antiquarian* that Putnam threatened libel against all who questioned the Gass discoveries.[8] There were also threats made against the Smithsonian, although none of that correspondence survives in Davenport. The existence of these threats is confirmed by Major John Wesley Powell, who mentioned it in 1890 in *The Forum*, a national literary magazine. He wrote on the subject of "Prehistoric Man in America." With an oblique reference to his colleague Henshaw and the threats made by Putnam, he remarked:

Not long ago a local society had in its possession two elephant pipes, the antiquity of which was questioned, in a passing sentence of an article, by one of the most skillful archaeologists of the country. Thereupon the society held meetings, and had their attorney make a careful investigation to see if the offending scientist could be successfully prosecuted for libel. And all this was in the interest of science, the high antiquity of man, and the exaltation of the ancient Mound-builders![9]

Powell's statements aroused a spirited reply in *The Naturalist,* a monthly publication of the Academy of Sciences in Kansas City. The full three columns of the front page, and another two on a back page, contained an article by Warren Watson entitled "Those Elephant Pipes Again." In this article, Watson denounced Major Powell for publishing untrue remarks and falsehoods:

> It is true these finds are unique and in this respect require great circumspection in their authentication; but this fact does not justify the brutal unfairness exhibited by Maj. Powell and his pseudo-archaeologist, Mr. Henshaw. . . . If the power placed in Maj. Powell's hands is to be misused and prostituted to the furtherance of his own hobbies, instead of the interests of science, a concerted action should be taken by all interested in scientific pursuits, looking to an investigation by Congress into the policy, methods and expenditures of the Bureau, to the end that the liberal sums appropriated from the public funds in aid of ethnological inquiries may not be diverted to the exploitation of personal hobbies and the aggrandizement of servile followers.[10]

Much of the language in this attack on the Smithsonian was taken from Putnam's defense of the unique Davenport specimens, well known because it had been widely distributed among private science academies. Powell's "hobby" was encouraging his "servile followers," particularly Cyrus Thomas, to resolve the Mound Builder question in American archaeology.

Whatever was involved in the attempted character assassinations of Tiffany, Lindley, Peet, Berlin, Stevens, Henshaw, Thomas, and Powell—it was not archaeology. Putnam had developed suspicions of such depth and intensity, and had planned such far-ranging attacks, that if any judgment is to be made of his character, it is to suggest that he might have benefited from medical treatment for his symptoms of paranoia.

12

THE OPPOSITION TICKET

Charles Putnam had defended the slate tablets and elephant pipes by employing legal tactics that might cast doubt on the stories told by those who knew the facts and legal threats to silence other critics. Putnam's publications emphasized reasonable doubt as to the solution of the mysterious origins of the relics; this was a successful tactic, which led many to regard the affair of the Mound Builders as an unsettled matter. But Putnam was allowed no rest in his labors to defend Reverend Gass and his startling discoveries. In January 1887 a new emergency arose. Putnam and his followers were confronted by dissident members, who vowed revenge for the expulsion and humiliation of A. S. Tiffany and Dr. Lindley. It became an organizational crisis of the greatest importance. If the dissidents were successful in their cause, every defense that Putnam had erected in print to shield the unique relics would be shattered.

The occasion of the new emergency was the usually humdrum, cut-and-dried election of new officers in the Academy. In January of 1887, Putnam was retiring as president; his handpicked successor was the first vice president, Charles Harrison, nicknamed "the stonecutter" by scoffers and locally renowned for his work at duplicating or creating artifacts. The "stonecutter" had worked with Gass at Mound 11 on the Cook Farm when the limestone tablet was uncovered, and Harrison had written up the report of the anomalous find, as has been explained.[1] Was it now appropriate to elect Harrison president of the Academy?

Those who had an intimate knowledge of the affair thought that the normal succession of first vice president to president should be

suspended in the case of Harrison, a man not well liked for his suspected complicity in the Gass affair and for helping to expel his
former comrades. To break the normal succession to higher office in
the Academy, the dissident members secretly organized themselves
into an opposition group. The extent of their success is one measure
of how widespread knowledge of the frauds was among local residents.

The plot against Harrison was organized by friends of Tiffany
and Lindley. They organized an attempted purge of the officers by
nominating local residents to membership, swelling the membership rolls. Next, at the January meeting, which few normally attended, they planned to all show up, present an alternative slate of
officers, and take over the Academy by storm. The purge of Harrison and other officers of the Academy upon the retirement of Putnam is described in the contemporary newspaper, the *Rock Island
Argus:*

> During the past year the academy has experienced a wonderful
> growth in membership; hardly a meeting has been held that
> applications were not made for initiation, and the society rather
> rejoiced than otherwise over its apparent prosperity.
>
> Suddenly, however, a bombshell was exploded, it revealed
> the reason for this unexplained growth, for back of it was seen
> the hands of the expelled members. They had adopted this un-
> derhand method of gaining the ascendancy by the votes of the
> new members, whose friends they were, and thus intruding
> themselves upon the society from which they had been expelled,
> and sounding the first notes of discord, which had not existed in
> the academy before.
>
> The discovery was made only a few weeks ago—but a short
> time before election. The members of the academy saw and real-
> ized the impending danger and saw too that in bringing out a
> full attendance on election night, the expelled members might
> be voted down. All the loyal members were notified and last
> night carriages were flying around as on occasion of a political
> election.
>
> The result of the annual election was the triumph of the
> academy, two to one, there being ninety-two members present
> out of whom the expelled members controlled thirty-one. Had
> not a full attendance been called out, however, the expelled
> members would probably have succeeded in their scheme.[2]

The opposition to the old leadership of Putnam, Harrison, and
Pratt had been very thorough, to the extent that they had *printed*

opposition ballots, cut for tearing off the individual names and putting the strips into the ballot box after nominating each candidate
from the floor in opposition to the official slate proposed by the
nominating committee. The curator, Pratt, saved one of the opposition ballots, printed and cut just like those prepared in advance by
the Putnam group.[3]

Although timely warning and carriages bringing in the members had finally overthrown the opposition, Putnam was furious
over the contested election of Harrison. From his law office in town,
Putnam wrote memos to Pratt demanding more information in order to take revenge. In one such memo to Pratt, dated 31 January
1887, Putnam wrote that "Mr. Harrison has justed handed me a
Rock Island Argus containing a very inaccurate account of our
meeting which gives occasion for correction."[4] It was the article that
has just been quoted. In his memo, Putnam required Pratt to provide detailed information on George French, a Lindley supporter
whose name had been proposed from the floor as president in opposition to Harrison's candidacy. The lawyer also began an investigation of the other eleven whose names appeared on the opposition
ballot as alternate candidates for officers and trustees.

On the basis of information received from Pratt and other
sources, Putnam published in the *Rock Island Argus* an explanation of his "belief that many excellent members voted with the
minority under an entire misapprehension as to the true state of
affairs."[5] Without naming Tiffany or Lindley, Putnam wrote that the
factional fight was waged by the two expelled members, "men who
had committed offenses of grave import." He next stated that it
"gives occasion for surprise that a movement so evidently revolu-
tionary in its character should have enlisted in its support some of
our most worthy citizens." Putnam labeled Tiffany and Lindley
"malcontents" who were "cunning and audacious." They had not
put their own names on the ballot but, according to Putnam's explanation, had circulated a petition among prominent businessmen, proposing for the opposition ticket men who rarely attended
and were not equipped to run the Academy. Two of them had not
even been consulted about having their names placed on the ballot.
Among the names of those proposed for trustees by the opposition,
Putnam had been enraged to discover that of Dr. Bowman, Lindley's
medical partner.

Putnam's newspaper attack could only have been written by a
nineteenth-century lawyer who had little fear of libel suits, for he
next provided a lengthy review of each of the twelve men on the

opposition ticket, giving exact details of their poor attendance records at various Academy functions. His attack on the dissidents in the *Rock Island Argus* concluded with the comment that he was writing all of this because it was his duty to the Academy "to make a plain statement of facts."

The January 1887 defeat of the opposition group in the clubroom election and the early February newspaper attack on those defeated was Putnam's final triumph. In the following June, the residence of Charles Putnam, which he had named "Woodlawn," burned to the ground on his eighteen-acre estate. Although there was no loss of life, the fire destroyed a large portion of Putnam's library, as well as all of his own literary manuscripts and those of his deceased son, Duncan. The fire was a bitter personal shock to the lawyer. He moved his family into a cottage on the estate grounds and planned to rebuild his mansion. Six weeks later, he died suddenly, presumably of a heart attack. He was sixty-three years old.

The Putnam family—there were seven surviving children—continued to take the greatest interest in the Davenport Academy, and Putnam's wife served as president for a term. A son, Edward K. Putnam, later became director of the successor to the Academy, the Davenport Museum, which was heavily endowed by his father. Renamed the Putnam Museum today, it is the largest and finest public museum in the state. There was another legacy as well: the Davenport conspiracy.

As a successful lawyer, Charles Putnam was accustomed to the exaggerated role of legal advocate who defends the guilty and innocent with equal fervor—magnifying discrepancies, proliferating arguments, and casting doubt upon all opponents and their witnesses. But to work, such advocacy required a courtroom with an equally vociferous prosecuting attorney, and there was none to fill that role in the Academy once the dissenters were expelled. By its courtroom tone, the conflict passed beyond scientific analysis of the specimens themselves and descended into an imbroglio. One of the unfortunate aspects of the case was the skill, personal magnetism, and possibly the convictions of the principal defender of the relics. Had he been less able, the controversy would have died and the truth would have come out at the time. Continued bitterness, errors, and confusion about the Davenport specimens survived long after the death of Charles Putnam, and in no small measure became his legacy to science.

Bringing in sixty elderly residents by carriages had blocked the opposition to Putnam, Harrison, and their friends, but after the Jan-

uary 1887 battle, the Academy was never the same again. Dating
from the disputed election of Harrison to the Academy presidency,
the membership greatly diminished in numbers, participation, and
activity; within a decade, the Academy had virtually disbanded,
having ceased to be a center of interest among the Yankees of
Davenport. Only the Putnam endowment kept the Academy alive,
making possible its transition to a public museum.

The minutes of meetings and manuscript records of hearings
provide vivid examples of the nonscientific goals and methods of
the Academy (and more generally illustrate the weaknesses of the
era of amateur contributors to science). In all the torrents of words
before committees and in meetings, none of the principals ever referred to the scientific publications of Henshaw, Thomas, Peet, or
Berlin—articles that provided such damning discussions of the
elephants and the tablets, and implicated Gass and others.

Why didn't the two "disgraced members" and their supporters
band together and found a rival academy of science? Why did they
attempt to take over the Davenport Academy through their membership drive? There is no question that Tiffany and Lindley were
seeking revenge against Putnam and his faction. The Academy, despite its pretensions, was not much of a scientific organization—it is
better described as a social club. The membership expelled the disgruntled members with trumped-up charges, as if they had been
caught cheating at cards.

No rival academy of science was formed because the whole notion of amateur research was obsolete in the 1880s. Besides, very
few Davenport citizens were interested in natural science. This fact
is abundantly clear from a study of the attendance records published from time to time in the Academy *Proceedings.*

In its heyday, the Davenport Academy often had no more than
four or five members attend the monthly meetings, which were organized by "sections" in geology, history, natural history, and archaeology. In the history section, two members met fairly regularly
and talked to each other about early Davenport memorabilia. In
geology, three or more gathered together and heard talks on collections and rock outcrops. In the early 1880s, Reverend Gass's section on archaeology sometimes drew as few as two other members
to hear his disquisitions on the mounds. A talk on two new plant
species from southern California by Dr. Parry brought out four other
members. Sometimes attendance rose dramatically to hear a talk
on some curiosity. Eighteen members turned out in the fall of 1879
to hear Dr. Lindley give a talk described as "an interesting, popular

paper on the boomerang." A glance at volume 3 of the *Proceedings*, which provides meeting notes, furnishes these examples of the relative lack of local involvement in scientific activity.

An analysis of membership lists at the end of 1881, the year before the scandal came to light, shows inflated rolls. The 434 members included 230 in an honorary group of nonresidents—most of them amateurs or part-time antiquarians, with a sprinkling of professional scientists—none of whom paid dues, receiving the *Proceedings* as a courtesy. Of 204 residents, at least 8 were deceased at the time the list was compiled; wives, husbands, and older children were listed separately, as one might list church membership to swell the rolls. For example, 9 Putnams were life members, and 4 Pratts were enrolled—the curator, his wife, and their two daughters. The list of separate surnames, excluding members known to be deceased, reduces the Academy membership in 1881 to 143, most of them inactive and many no longer paying dues. Among those remaining, the Academy was considered to be a worthy enough cause to support with dues at three dollars per year. However, only 53 felt sufficiently involved to contribute to the building fund of 1877–78, although for a contribution of five dollars, one's name was printed on the list of donors. Science, even amateur science, did not have that much general interest for the residents of Midwest communities, then as now.

The disgruntled minority could not organize a rival academy because there were no amateur scientists beyond a handful of middle-aged and elderly men, most of whom were dead by the 1890s. For the most part, the local contributions to the *Proceedings* were written by dabblers. Early volumes contained a stream of meeting notes, announcements, resolutions, and local members' scientific observations on mound relics, lightning phenomena, paleontological specimens, or such questions as whether rifle balls burn upon impact. Volume 5, covering the years 1885–89, is the last of this type of *Proceedings*. Volume 6 still contains minutes of meetings, but the scientific papers were contributed by professional scientists. Later volumes discontinued the minutes and the chance to see one's name in print, and the series finally became an outlet for publishing natural history theses from the University of Iowa. It ceased publication altogether in 1910.

The opposition ticket and the factionalism of 1886–87 came at the very time when amateur research was abandoned as unprofitable at the Academy. The amateur-academy type of organization was meanwhile losing ground as local groups disbanded across the

United States. In Iowa, the Des Moines Academy became extinct, the Muscatine Academy disappeared, and the Sioux City Academy gave up around 1904. The sole survivor was the Iowa City Academy, its life prolonged by University of Iowa faculty, until it became transformed into the statewide Iowa Academy of Science, its city connection long since forgotten. The academy organization of amateur research had lived beyond its intellectual means by the 1880s, and with the exception of the Iowa City group, the only survivors became museums, where research was unimportant.

13

EVIDENCE OF THE FRAUDS

In 1894 the Bureau of American Ethnology finally issued the long-delayed report on mound explorations by Cyrus Thomas.[1] This monograph described the findings at hundreds of mounds excavated by assistants working for the Bureau, research carried out in almost all major regions of eastern North America and the Midwest. The importance of the report lay in its method of dealing with the vexing question of mound origins. Speculations about lost races of Mound Builders had run almost unchecked for a century, and Thomas evaluated the controversy with scientific evidence. Other studies had appeared previously, but the 1894 monograph was seven hundred pages long and so detailed that it convinced professional anthropologists and archaeologists that the matter was finally settled.

Major Powell wrote an introduction to this huge monograph, the most important single study on American archaeology that had appeared up to that time. In it, Powell said it was difficult to exaggerate the prevalence of the romantic fallacy that lost races superior to the Indians had once lived on the continent:

> The forest-covered mounds have been usually regarded as the mysterious sepulchers of its kings and nobles. It was an alluring conjecture that a powerful people, superior to the Indians, once occupied the valley of the Ohio and the Appalachian ranges, their empire stretching from Hudson Bay to the Gulf, with its flanks on the western prairies and the eastern ocean; a people with a confederated government, a chief ruler, a great central

capital, a highly developed religion, with homes and
husbandry . . . with a language, perhaps with letters, all swept
away before an invasion of copperhued Huns from some unknown region of the earth, prior to the landing of Columbus.[2]

Powell next described the scientific evidence that refuted such
grandiose speculations. It could be shown that some of the mounds
had been built by Indians in historic times because they contained
glass beads and typical European trade goods. Other artifacts found
in these post-Columbian mounds were like those found in more ancient mounds. This study of artifact types showed that there had
been continuity in the mound tradition and provided the inescap-
able conclusion that the ancestors of those Indians seen by the explorers were responsible for the prehistoric earthworks.

The most conspicuous data pointing the other way, to the existence of lost races, were the Davenport and the Grave Creek tablets.
Both examples were dismissed by Cyrus Thomas, who repeated the
arguments previously published in *Science.* However, his summary
carried greater weight because the large-scale excavations had
found no parallels to the unique relics.[3]

On a local level, many continued to accept the possible genuineness of the tablets, particularly the elephant pipes. The affair became muddled. In the 1890s, Frederick Starr, a founder of the
American Anthropological Association, insisted that the Davenport
specimens were an open question despite the publication of the
monograph by Thomas. Stephen Peet repeatedly wrote that the
elephant pipes seemed to be genuine. After the turn of the century,
the beginning of scientific archaeology in Iowa was spurred on by
the hope that more elephant pipes might be found. Even in the
1920s, Clark Wissler of the American Museum and Charles Keyes,
who founded the Iowa Archaeological Survey, did not consider the
unique relics to be frauds.[4]

In large measure, such hopes were nurtured by the lack of a
definitive study of the specimens. The first examination was made
by Dr. Henry Shetrone, director of the Ohio State Museum and at
that time probably the most knowledgeable American archaeologist
on Hopewell culture. He came because of an invitation extended by
the director of the Davenport Museum, Edward K. Putnam, son of
the redoubtable Charles Putnam. The tablets were no longer at issue, but there remained a belief that the elephant pipes might be
genuine, and in any event, the director wished to have an honest
professional opinion.

Shetrone's report was a three-part manuscript that included a covering statement, detailed memoranda describing the various pipes, and catalog notes.[5] He studied all of the platform pipes in the Davenport collection and concluded that only thirty-one of sixty-five conformed to his criteria for genuineness. This was an astonishing conclusion, for it clearly supported the charges made by Dr. Lindley that frauds were commonplace. Shetrone was unaware of the manuscripts giving the detailed statements by Lindley, and he reached his conclusions from objective examinations of the specimens. At the time I made my examination of the pipes in 1969, only forty-four remained in the museum's collection, but by making use of the earlier study, it is possible to reconstruct information on the lost specimens.

In general I concurred with Shetrone's identifications. He stated that the elephant pipes had been soaked in grease to give them an appearance of age, and he also noted shoe polish or a similar material on another pipe.[6] The remaining fabrications did not conform to specifications in material, shape, techniques, or proportions characteristic of Hopewellian specimens. He made no effort to identify the sources of the frauds. Edward Putnam found out what he wished to know about the matter, and the manuscript by Shetrone was carefully filed away rather than published, for the *Proceedings* had been dormant for twenty years. Neither man made any effort to publish the conclusions elsewhere.

We will now do a little detective work on the pipes, based upon my own evaluation. Who was responsible for introducing the frauds into the Davenport Academy collections? The catalog notes list the excavator or purchaser of each of the sixty-five pipes, for in those days interesting specimens were bought from private collectors who claimed to have found them in mounds. Sometimes this was true and sometimes it was not. It turned out to be a very bad practice, for it encouraged plundering of archaeological sites, established a marketplace for antiquities, and caused unscrupulous men to manufacture frauds in order to make a profit. Museums and professional archaeological societies no longer consider the purchase of specimens to be an ethical practice.

From the specimen catalog, I made a list showing who gave or sold each of the pipes to the Academy. From Shetrone's notes and my own study, I also knew whether each pipe was genuine or fraudulent. (See Tables A.1–A.3 in the appendix.) When I combined this information, it showed a pattern of deception which was so clear that it startled me (Table 13.1).

Table 13.1. *Pipe specimens and their finders/donors*

Genuine pipes	Fraudulent pipes	Finder or donor
14	12	Jacob Gass
0	2	Adolph Blumer
0	15	Edwin Gass
16	0	Academy members and field parties
0	2	Miscellaneous gifts
1	3	No information
31	34	Total

The Gass family was responsible for at least twenty-nine of the thirty-four frauds. Edwin Gass emerges in an important role, for he donated no genuine pipes and fifteen frauds. Sometimes he said he "found" them, and on one occasion, he was at an excavation when his brother retrieved a fraud. Six pipes allegedly came from Muscatine, and the others were from Rock Island and Mercer counties in Illinois. Edwin was not a member of the Academy, and his name rarely appeared in the *Proceedings*. His activities were not mentioned in the Tiffany and Lindley hearings.

Reverend Edwin Gass, a Lutheran clergyman, never succeeded in finding a pulpit. Apparently very short of money, Edwin moved in with Jacob Gass in Postville and could do no better than find a job as saloonkeeper before returning to Switzerland. Personal financial problems may best explain his role in selling fraudulent artifacts.

Reverend Blumer, the brother-in-law, "excavated" the second elephant pipe and was present on another occasion when a grease-soaked limestone pipe was found by Jacob Gass. By implication, it appears that Reverend Gass was imposed upon by his own family, possibly motivated by jealousy over the fame he had achieved as a mound digger.

Jacob Gass himself gave fourteen genuine pipes to the Academy and obtained some others by purchase. However, he was not very discriminating, and twelve fraudulent pipes passed into the Academy collections during the course of his excavations and purchases. Some of the frauds came from excavated sites previously visited by the omnipresent janitor, John Graham, who sometimes helped him locate mounds.

Field trips sponsored by the Academy and gifts from members added sixteen genuine pipes to the collections in the museum. No frauds have been detected among this group of specimens. Persons associated with these donations included Lindley, Tiffany, French, Harrison, Pratt, Hall, and others. From this information, one can understand why so many Academy members considered the statements by Lindley and Tiffany to be slanderous.

The dates of discovery are of interest. The early work by Jacob Gass produced all genuine pipes and no frauds. The first elephant pipe found in 1878 marks the beginning of frauds introduced into the collections of the Academy, a year after the slate tablets came to light at the Cook Farm. During the next five years, the frauds continued at an accelerating rate, climaxing in the fifteen frauds donated by Edwin Gass in the spring of 1883, when the Gass family left Davenport. This donation was described in both the *Proceedings* and *Science*.[7] All pipes obtained later were genuine.

The makers of frauds preferred to create effigy pipes rather than the plain, unadorned type, which had less market value. Genuine effigy pipes were rare, most of the finds being the plain type; the normal percentage of frequency was reversed among the fakes (Table 13.2). Not only is the percentage of effigy types suspiciously large among the fakes, but as Shetrone pointed out in his manuscript, the frauds were usually made from the wrong material; the platforms are crude with rounded edges, and they lack the graceful proportions and balance of the genuine specimens. We will consider these characteristics.

Table 13.2. *Genuine and forged platform pipes*

	Effigy	Plain	Total
Genuine	7 (23%)	24 (77%)	31
Fraudulent	23 (68%)	11 (32%)	34

The material provides a striking contrast between the genuine and the spurious artifacts. The genuine pipestone is described by Shetrone as: "familiar greenish-drab flinty fire clay, ordinarily known as 'pipestone.' This material, which is readily and positively identifiable, was the favorite material of the Hopewellians throughout the area of their occurrence, and probably was used in the manufacture of 95 percent of all known pipes. . . . The flinty fire clay occurs definitely in Scioto County, Ohio, where ancient quarries exist, and doubtless in numerous other localities in the Middle West."[8] I know of no such quarries in Iowa. The genuine pipes were clearly made of imported Ohio pipestone, or in rarer cases, of material brought to the state from the west. Such imports rarely occurred in Iowa during the Hopewellian period, and pipes are seldom found, although Hopewellian pottery is more common. From this fact, we now know that all of the mound pillaging seldom succeeded in obtaining genuine pipes, because of their rarity. Reverend Jacob Gass was very fortunate in his choice of the Cook Farm mound group. Other members of the Davenport Academy that excavated along the Mississippi in Iowa and Illinois seldom found such specimens. This led to jealousy and suspicion on the part of some of the members, which led in turn to the tablet hoaxes, designed to make a fool of the clergyman. It was this jealousy, along with greed, that drove Edwin Gass and Adolph Blumer to perpetrate frauds on their relative.

A geologist, J. N. Young, assisted me in the study of the forty-four pipes still remaining in the museum collection, and she identified the different materials from which the pipes were made (Table 13.3). The frauds were made from red ferruginous shale, clay, limestone, and other materials close at hand. One fraudulent pipe was made from a genuine pipe material, red catlinite, which possibly came from the famous southwestern Minnesota pipestone quarry. This fox-shaped pipe (figure 13.5b) was given by Edwin Gass. The pipe blank (figure 13.7g), unfinished but roughed out to an approximate pipe form, is problematic. Both the *Proceedings* and Shetrone termed it limestone, but microscopic evaluation by J. N. Young showed that it was probably welded tuff, possibly from Yellowstone. This pipe was donated by a man named Parsons, who does not seem to be part of the group of fraudulent-pipe makers. Shetrone considered this unfinished pipe to be a fraud because he misidentified the material as limestone, but I have tentatively grouped it with the genuine specimens. Both elephant pipes (figures 13.1a and 13.1b) were made from limestone, which was readily available to the forgers, who made many pipes from this stone. The next most popular material appears to have been fired clay, which could be modeled into shape by the forgers without the laborious use of hand tools.

Table 13.3. Pipe material

Genuine pipes	Examples	Fraudulent pipes	Examples
Green Ohio pipestone	14	Limestone	9
Red and Green pipestone	1	Red ferruginous shale	4
Red pipestone	1	Clay (?)	6
Calcite	2	Talc	3
Welded tuff	1	Sandstone	1
		Red catlinite	1
		Argillite or slate (?)	1
Total	19		25

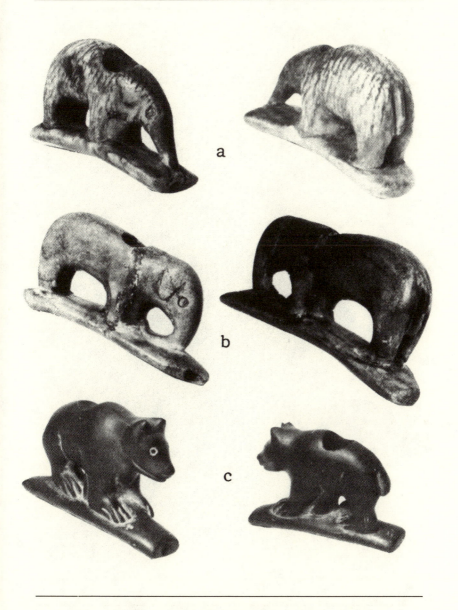

13.1.   *Platform pipe frauds: (a, b) elephants, (c) bear. (Putnam Museum specimens)*

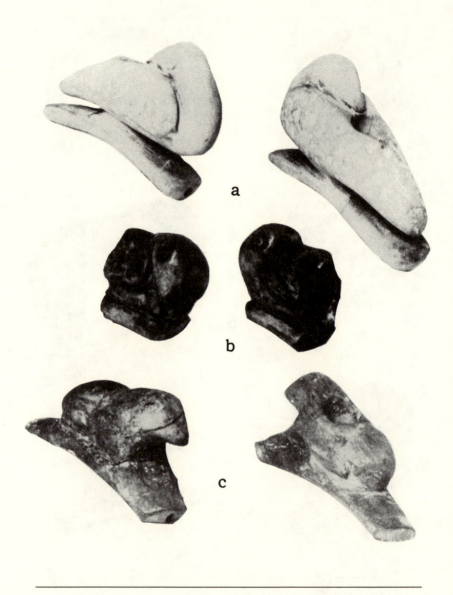

a

b

c

13.2.   *Platform pipe frauds: (a) swan, (b) bird, (c) animal. (Putnam*
Museum specimens)

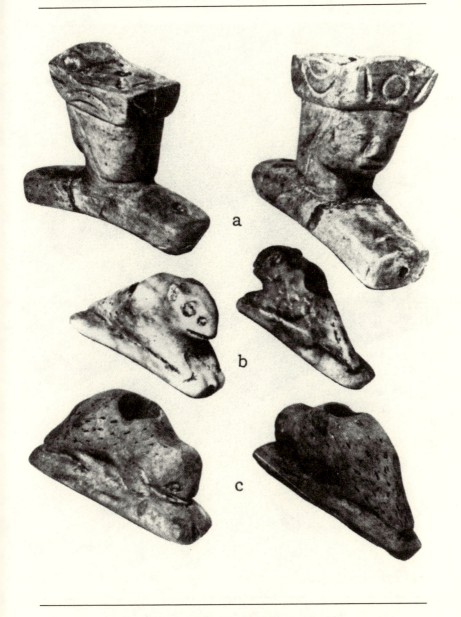

13.3.   *Platform pipe frauds: (a) human head, (b, c) beavers(?). (Putnam Museum specimens)*

13.4. Platform pipe frauds: (a) howling wolf, (b) lizard, (c) turtle.
(Putnam Museum specimens)

112

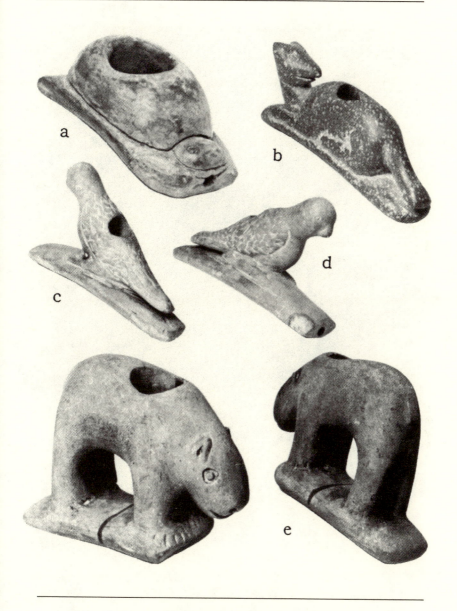

13.5.　*Platform pipe frauds:* (a) *beetle,* (b) *fox,* (c, d) *birds,* (e) *bear.*
(Putnam Museum specimens)

13.6. Platform pipe frauds: (a, b, c, e, f, g) plain, (d, h) animals.
(Putnam Museum specimens)

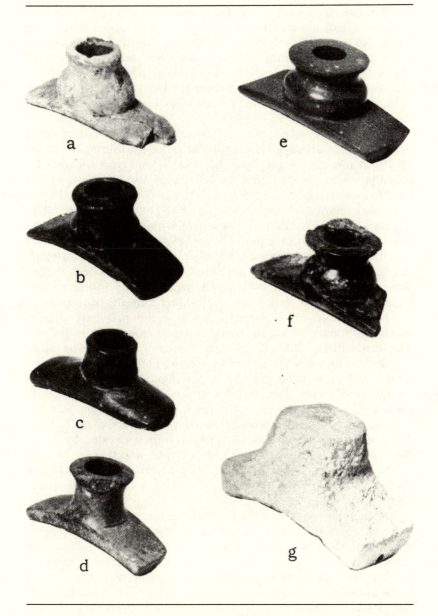

13.7. "Genuine" plain platform pipes, however, the authenticity of the pipe blank (g) has been questioned. (Putnam Museum specimens)

Patination, or weathering, is present on many of the genuine specimens, but not on all of them. Some were cleaned after being found. No true weathering is present on any of the spurious specimens. During his examination, Shetrone removed various kinds of film or finish used to hide the marks of recent manufacture, superficial coatings that were no longer present when I examined the specimens in 1969. Shoe blacking covered fresh stone on the so-called howling wolf pipe (figure 13.4a) and a plain bowl specimen, now missing. A thick, black, gummy substance, which had partially peeled off upon drying, exposed fresh stone on the lizard pipe (figure 13.4b). A metallic coating, possibly from a lead pencil, covered a lizard pipe now missing from the collection. And oil or grease was used to give an appearance of age on six other specimens, including the two elephants (see figures 13.1a and 13.1b), a broken bird effigy (figure 13.2b), and an animal variously termed a seal or otter but possibly an attempt to depict a beaver (figure 13.3b). Two missing specimens similarly treated with oil or grease were a swan effigy and a plain platform pipe. An unknown paste substance that Shetrone washed or brushed off covered fresh incisions on a swan pipe (figure 13.2a) and a plain pipe now missing from the collection.

Furthermore, fire was used to mask freshly prepared surfaces on six specimens, all but the turtle being donations of Edwin Gass. The turtle (figure 13.4c) was also treated with glue. The other burned specimens were two amorphous animals (figures 13.2c and 13.6h) and three plain platform pipes (figures 13.6a, 13.6b, and 13.6g). And finally, four fraudulent specimens were apparently carved with a jackknife from a ferruginous red shale, almost a hematite, which was easily worked. No effort was made to conceal the fresh incisions. Two of these specimens were excavated by Jacob Gass, one was donated by his brother Edwin, and there is no data on the fourth one. One of the four pipes represents an animal (figure 13.6d), and the remainder are plain (figures 13.6c, 13.6e, and 13.6f).

Although a number of different indices could be applied to illustrate the differences between the genuine and the spurious pipes, I shall limit the discussion to three types of measurements taken during my study of the collection. The hole diameter of the pipe stem is one significant measurement because of the use of modern drills to make the frauds. I obtained a complete set of drill bits in 1/64-inch increments and matched them to the pipe stem holes, the match being made when the butt or smooth end of the bit fitted snugly when pushed through the opening in the bowl. In studying

the specimens, I used inches rather than metric measurements because that was the system used in the forgeries (Table 13.4).

It would appear that a ³/₃₂-inch drill bit was the favorite of the
forgers, particularly if one also counts the five specimens with the
next larger size (as would be justified by drill wear enlarging the
hole). Such a drill bit would then fit 78 percent of the specimens.
Two of the frauds did not even have a stem hole, and the apparently
genuine blank was not drilled out. In contrast, the genuine pipes
tended to have slightly larger stem holes than the frauds and
showed more variation, as one would expect with hand workman-
ship.

A common feature of the genuine specimens is a bowl hole vertical to the platform. This is almost an invariable trait; among the
sample, there is only one exception. The forgers of the spurious
pipes did not study the genuine pipes very closely, and they drilled
out the bowl holes carelessly, usually at an angle to the pipe platform. Among genuine pipes, 95 percent of the sample have vertical
holes, compared with 20 percent of the frauds.

When some of the less sophisticated amateurs made pipes, they
conceived of them as they were illustrated in contemporary publications, which were usually in side profiles. In consequence, they un-
derestimated the width of the platform found on genuine specimens. It is possible to express this mathematically by a very simple
ratio: maximum length divided by maximum width multiplied by
100. Measurements were taken and the ratio index determined for
each complete pipe. The results of this comparison showed that the
index for the genuine pipes ranged from 5.0 to 3.6 in 95 percent of
the cases, but only 20 percent of the frauds conformed to this index.
Expressed another way, the length of the platform on the genuine
pipes was little more than twice as long as the width. The fake pipes
generally had a length that was closer to three times the width of

Table 13.4.   Minimum pipe-stem hole diameters

Diameter (¹/₆₄ inches)	Fraudulent pipes		Genuine pipes	
9	0		1	(5.5%)
8	1	(4%)	6	(33.0%)
7	5	(22%)	6	(33.0%)
6	13	(56%)	4	(22.0%)
5	3	(13%)	0	—
4	1	(4%)	1	(5.5%)
Total	23		18	

the platform, another indication of the lack of attention to detail on the part of the forgers.

The various observations considered here indicate that the frauds can be readily set apart from the genuine pipes. To summarize, the frauds were made with narrow platforms and bowl holes that were not vertical to the base, and most of their stem holes were drilled with a ³/₁₆-inch steel bit. Over one-third of the frauds were smeared with grease, oil, gum, lead pencil, shoe blacking, or other common household material to hide freshly worked surfaces. Six others were burned for the same purpose. At least four others still bore marks of the jackknife used to make them. The remaining specimens had little or no surface treatment to mask the recent fabrication of the limestone, clay, and other stone used in the frauds. If these specimens seem obvious today, it must finally be explained that during the 1880s, the criteria for genuineness were less well known.

The tablets lay at the center of the controversy, and Dr. Lindley's remarks about them are very pertinent because of his information about the activities of the Academy members. According to the minutes of the general Academy meeting, Dr. Lindley defended himself by saying:

> Everyone who knew anything about ancient relics knew these tablets to be recent. Any stone-cutter would say so. Anybody who knew anything about glue and cement would say so. The man who helped find them [presumed to be John Hume] said the account of their finding was not true. The man who owned the farm upon which the mound was located said it was not true. Everybody knew that bogus relics were manufactured from time to time in various places. These relics were, as everybody agreed, manufactured. We had a man in the area who boasted he could make such things. Anybody could draw the conclusions.[9]

The Cremation Scene tablet, approximately 12 inches by 9½ inches, was broken to hide the nail holes. It was subsequently smashed during the excavation and repaired. It was almost immediately encased in plaster with a wooden frame, and I was not given permission to remove a thin section of it in order to definitely establish the origin of the material. (The photograph in figure 2.5 was taken shortly after the discovery and before the tablet was framed.) At the time of discovery, the material was identified as black shale, which was assumed to be a local material. But black shale does not occur in east central Iowa. The material actually appears to be New England or Michigan slate, which was used in the nineteenth century as building material; specifically, expensive buildings frequently had slate roof tiles, and ornamental slate-tile sheathing in different sizes, patterns, and colors was sometimes used to cover vertical wall sections of Victorian-period buildings. This slate sheathing usually occurred near the roof on a second or third story. It was rarely used on the first story of buildings because slates within reach of the ground were frequently vandalized. The slates were easily broken off and were expensive to replace. Slate work represented a specialized craft in nineteenth-century construction. One of the rare buildings in Davenport that had lower-story slate siding was the Old Slate House, and this siding was the alleged source of the Davenport tablets. According to the Hurlbut transcript (see chapter 14), the slates were broken off and carved by a group of Academy members.

The letters and characters forming the inscription seem to have been copied from some readily available reference. The Hurlbut transcript states that two almanacs, one German and the other Hebrew, provided the inspiration, and the letters were drawn at random without any intent to spell out words. There are a few characters that might have been Hebrew characters, but there is no preponderance of letters from such a source. It would seem that Cyrus Thomas was nearer the mark when he pointed out striking resemblances between many of the characters and those appearing in the table of comparative alphabets in the 1872 edition of *Webster's Dictionary*. Indications of a modern source of origin for the inscription include the occurrence of a mixture of letters and numbers. Greek letters include pi, upsilon, psi, and delta; Roman letters are *f, d, o, w,* and cruder examples of *h, u,* and *y.* There are other examples of characters that add to the confusion, among which are two ampersands and two examples of the musical clef sign (see figure 2.7). Arabic 8s and possible Roman numerals also occur. It was not a sophisticated forgery, and the diverse elements support the claims made by some Academy members that it was intended as a joke.

I emphasize here that modern symbolism appears on the tablets. The zodiac is ancient Near Eastern in origin, but the "sign" symbols did not come into use until the Early Renaissance. Small or lowercase Greek letters are of no greater antiquity. Musical notation symbolism found on the Cremation Scene can be no earlier than the seventeenth or more likely eighteenth century. Mathematical notation is equally recent: Particular attention is called to the ∺ geometric proportion sign in the upper right-hand corner of the inscription. Amateur scientists would have been familiar with this symbol even without using *Webster's Dictionary* or any other source for reference.

The Hunting Scene tablet is the reverse side of the Cremation Scene, for the two sides had separated along a cleavage plane. The illustration (figure 2.6) was prepared very soon after the discovery, and it was later encased in plaster and framed. Among various interpretations, some thought they saw the Tree of Life and the Noachian Deluge portrayed by the crudely drawn human and animal figures. A sophisticated hoax would have left no doubt about the biblical scene intended. The random, shallow incisions show that the forgers did not spend much time on this side of the tablet and that they used a sharp steel blade, such as a jackknife. The most crudely drawn animals are problematic. Three were identified as she moose or even possible representations of elephants, although no example is very clear. Some of the animals are not native to the Midwest, among them seals, which also appeared on effigy-pipe frauds.

The Calendar tablet (figures 2.4 and 6.3) is actually a zodiac copied from *Webster's Dictionary* or an almanac. The circles were drawn with a steel compass, which left a central pit. The specimen is clearly an unaltered slate shingle 6¾ inches square with two suspension or nail holes, each measuring ⅜ inches in diameter. Other modern dimensions are the diameters of the circles, inscribed in sizes of 2, 3½, 5, and 6¼ inches. The distances between the circles measure about ¾ of an inch.

The limestone tablet with the Indian figure was broken at the time of excavation and later repaired. The tablet measures 7 by 12 inches and is 1½ inches thick. The Indian, axe, and pipes were brightly painted with red ochre at the time of discovery. The photograph taken shortly after discovery shows the quartz eyes still glued in place on the two bird-effigy pipes (figure 4.2). They later disappeared. It may be that the Indian also had quartz eyes, and these came unglued at the time of excavation. Both a Roman VIII and an Arabic 8 appear on this tablet discovered by Charles Harrison and Reverend Gass in 1878 (see figure 6.2). The other shallow incisions closely resemble marks on the Cremation Scene slate tablet, including a square with a dot inside. The limestone with a neatly dressed edge on the left side is said to have come from Schmidt's Quarry nearby.

Dr. Lindley's remarks about cement and glue become clearer when one compares the concretion (figure 13.8) with the limestone tablet. The concretion was found in the back dirt of Mound 3 at the Cook Farm after Jacob Gass completed his excavation for the slate tablets. Cyrus Thomas pointed out that this linked the discovery of the slate tablets with the limestone tablet from Mound 11, because of the quartz eyes on both specimens. No quartz inserts have ever been found on genuine artifacts. The two views of the concretion are taken from the *Proceedings*, since the quartz is now missing from the specimen.

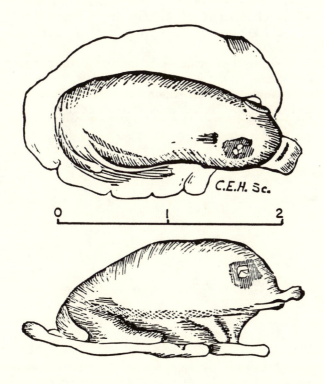

13.8.   A natural concretion to which quartz eyes had been added (scale in inches added). The quartz was glued with white cement or glue, but is now missing. (Harrison 1880:256–57; Putnam Museum specimen AR-15092)

The tablets were found in two Cook Farm mounds that had previously been disturbed. This fact led professional archaeologists—among them Foreman, Thomas, and Peet—to the conclusion that the tablets were intrusive or "planted." The illustration of Mound 3 shows grave A, excavated by Reverend Gass in 1874, with undisturbed burials (see figure 3.1). Grave B is the adjacent burial pit, which he excavated in 1877, finding the slate tablets among scattered and incomplete human bones. Foreman termed burial pit B "thoroughly ransacked," meaning that someone had dug it up and planted the slate tablets and concretion prior to Reverend Gass's excavation. Both vertical and cross-sectional views of Mound 3 were published in the *Proceedings of the Davenport Academy.* A cross-sectional plan of Mound 11 also showed disturbance. The cavity in the ground beneath the stone altar indicated to Cyrus Thomas and subsequent archaeologists that the tablet had been put in the mound only a short time before Harrison, Hume, and Jacob Gass unearthed it again.

This is the physical evidence of the frauds that so perplexed many antiquarians in the late 1870s and 1880s. There is one last aspect of the tangled case, an evaluation of local tradition about the controversy that has survived in the Davenport area.

14

HOW A JUDGE CONTRIBUTED
TO LEGEND

In 1947 John H. Bailey, director of the Davenport Museum and a man interested in local archaeology, gave a talk to his fellow members of the Contemporary Club of Davenport. This group, restricted by its bylaws to thirty-three regular members (who called themselves "the immortals" in their sessions), existed as an organization from about 1895 until it became extinct in the mid-1960s. Such a talk would have been forgotten except for the club tradition of printing a yearly report that included everyone's paper. Because of the small size of the membership, one could fairly say that Bailey's speech about the Davenport affair belongs to that ephemeral class of manuscripts that have been printed but not published, for it was never reprinted nor even cited in any other publication. The Davenport Museum had no copy of it, and the only known original report is in the Special Collections of the Davenport Public Library.[1] John Bailey never published a fuller, corrected version or included a bibliography. In 1948 he committed suicide by hanging himself from the water pipes in the basement of the old Academy building, a matter that gave rise to considerable gossip unrelated to his exposure of the frauds.[2]

In his talk to the Contemporary Club, Bailey informally summarized the discovery and debates over the tablets and elephants. He titled his discussion "An Unsolved Davenport Mystery" because the perpetrator of the forgeries was not known to him:

As in all mystery stories the search for "who-done-it" is the main objective and always the author has the answer in the last chapter. In this case, we shall have to be different—for the name of the culprit, if such he may be called, is still unknown; and therein lies the mystery. All the participants in the case, which focused the eyes of the scientific world upon Davenport, have long since passed away. At this late date, the clues are gone and all that remains are the objects in question themselves, and the various reports on them which are to be found in all the scientific libraries of the world.

Bailey continued with his view that the maker of these objects "either had a grudge against the Academy or he wished, because he was a friend of the Academy that it should be the first to show the world actual remains proving the contemporaneousness of the mound builder and the mastodon." As for the role of Reverend Jacob Gass, Bailey wrote, "What better person to find his frauds and announce them to the world could the faker have chosen than a man of God whose integrity was unquestioned? Especially when that minister spent every free moment digging in the mounds. . . . In all sincerity Gass believed in his finds, and as I have pointed out—he was merely a means to an end."[3]

After giving this talk, Bailey learned that his "unsolved mystery" had a solution and that each of his previous surmises was wrong. The object of the hoax was neither to aid nor detract from the Davenport Academy but was aimed at making a fool of Gass himself. The clues were not gone, for there were documents within his own museum. Nor had all of the participants' knowledge passed away, for there was still a local tradition that lingered on in the 1940s. Gass may have believed in his finds "in all sincerity" at first, but he eventually learned the truth. He was not merely a "means to an end"; Gass was, if I may twist a phrase, the end of the means. The story of how Bailey learned the solution, too late to include it in the posthumously circulated 1948 summary of the case, is contained in the Hurlbut transcript.

I had learned from Donald Herold that there was an oral tradition about the Davenport frauds, and when I later made my investigation, I was directed by Carol Hunt of the museum staff to visit Irving Hurlbut. I was familiar with his name as a knowledgeable amateur archaeologist, and in March 1969 I met him for the first time. He was born in Muscatine, and his family subsequently moved to Davenport, where he grew up and lived for fifty years. He was an auditor at the Union Savings Bank of Davenport, and after

his retirement in the mid-1950s, he moved back to Muscatine. At
the time I met with him, he was a justice of the peace and ran a
small tourist shop selling rocks, minerals, and artifacts. While employed in Davenport, Mr. Hurlbut knew various directors and
worked as a volunteer for the museum. Over a period of twenty
years, he went on field trips with various directors, collected information on Indian mounds, and helped with the excavations. On
some occasions, he assisted with the museum exhibits. I mention
these biographical details because Mr. Hurlbut was a reliable local
source of information.

At the time of my visit, I was accompanied by J. N. Young, who
had previously met him in connection with the geology of the area.
We made a written record of the discussion, reviewed it, and sent
the typed copy back to him for corrections and additions. The story
Mr. Hurlbut told was not a firsthand account but one that had been
told to him by Judge James Wills Bollinger of Davenport. I will
present it here as it was given to me on a Sunday afternoon in
March in the living room of Mr. Hurlbut's home.

> Judge Bollinger lived on East Locust Street in Davenport
> and his hobby was the study of Abraham Lincoln. He was highly
> respected all over town. The late John Bailey, former Director of
> the Davenport Museum and I were always together. The Judge
> figured we knew the entire history of the archaeology of Scott
> County and so he said to us, "The doctor told me I have only six
> months to live and I wanted somebody to know about the Daven-
> port tablets and pipes." He invited both of us to have lunch with
> him at his hideaway in the Chamber of Commerce Building lo-
> cated at the N.W. corner of 4th and Main Streets. He said to the
> waiter when he came to his private room, "Bring us three of the
> usual." Neither Bailey nor I were what you would call drinking
> men and we were just dumbfounded at their size. These were
> followed by a delicious dinner. It was then that he told us the
> story. . . . I will try to put it in the Judge's words as I remember
> them.
>
> The Judge told us: "We had no respect for Reverend Gass
> because he was the biggest windjammer and liar and everyone
> knew he was. We wanted to shut him up once and for all. So I
> went down to the Old Slate House and went to the back of the
> building where nobody could see what I was doing and tore off a
> number of the old slates. The entire building was covered with
> slates. I took the slates up to the Academy basement where the
> old gang met.
>
> "Well this group would go to the Academy and have a bull
> session because there wasn't anyplace else to go. They used to

have a few drinks and just shoot the breeze. The janitor was in with us. We had two old almanacs, one German and one Hebrew, and we copied out of them and inscribed the hieroglyphics on those slate tablets, and things we just made up—anything that would confuse them, especially Gass.

"That fall Gass was digging down at the Cook Mounds. Cold weather had just set in and we knew Gass wouldn't dig anymore 'til spring. So we carved the slate tablet and several of the pipes and to make the pipes look old we covered them with oil that was on the janitor's workbench. He had more time to work on these things than we did.

"Then some of the boys went up to Tiffany's house because we knew he had a collection of minerals. Tiffany wasn't home at the time but to be sure everyone knew it was a joke, his wife gave us one of his best quartz crystals, one that Gass had seen many times and admired. She thought it was a pretty good joke. The shell and red ocher we got from the museum.

"We went over to Schmidt's Quarry and carried the pieces of limestone and built a little pyramid over the tablet and crystal and shell. The shell was from the Gulf of Mexico. We knew in the spring of the year he'd start digging again.

"Sure enough he went down there again when the weather warmed and came back with the stuff and we just shut up and let him rave and rant.

"First thing we knew the unusual find was published in Europe as well as in this country and spread like wildfire. By then it was too late to say anything about it. Tiffany wouldn't even admit at the time that it was his crystal, but later on of course he admitted it.

"I just wanted somebody to know it was all a fake. It was all made in the basement. We were all in on it."

Judge Bollinger at the time said, "I still have those old slates in the basement of my house. Come up some time and get all of them. Get them all out of here. At the same time I'll show you my Lincoln collection. I've just completed arrangements with the State of Iowa to give it to the University and it will be the last time you will get a chance to see it.

I went up to his house to get the slate pieces and he said, "Take the whole bunch. Get them out of here."

There were a number of them in an old bushel basket, perhaps a dozen. I still have some of them. You can see nail holes in some of them, just like the nail holes in one of the tablets.[4]

Mr. Hurlbut gave the University of Iowa Archaeological Laboratory the slate shingle he had in his living room, and it has a nail hole with the same diameter as those on the Calendar stone: ³⁄₈ inch (compare the shingle, figure 14.1, with the Calendar stone in figure 2.4). The other tablets from Judge Bollinger were in storage.

At the time the Hurlbut transcript was recorded, I had read the museum archives and the publications and had gained a thorough knowledge of the case. There were some loose ends that needed to be tied up, and so there were questions and answers included in the transcript that can be summarized here. I was curious about the location of some of the places mentioned in the Bollinger account. The Old Slate House was a well-known "sporting house," a euphemism in former use for a house of prostitution. It was said to be very well known to travelers, for it was located on the riverfront at the Davenport entrance to Government Bridge. Mississippi steamboats often tied up in front of the old Slate House.[5] Schmidt's quarry, the source of the limestone tablet, was located about one thousand feet northwest of the Cook mounds and was part of the Cook Farm when Reverend Gass and his associates conducted their excavations. Hurlbut explained that the water-filled quarry could still be seen on

14.1. *The judge's gift from the Old Slate House. Irving Hurlbut said this slate roofing shingle was given to him by Judge Bollinger to confirm the story that the slate tablets came from a notorious local house of prostitution. (University of Iowa, State Archaeologist's Laboratory 199–1, contributed by Irving Hurlbut)*

the road to Credit Island, east of the road after crossing the railroad tracks. At the present time, the Cook Farm mound site is covered by the building of the Thompson-Hayward Chemical Company, 2040 W. River Street. In the 1870s, this was a rural area known as Cook's Point on the Mississippi River. The river was some thousand feet east of the mounds, with a creek to the west.

Another group of questions and answers concerned the principal members of the Academy who were in on the hoax. Who, in fact, were the "old gang" who met in the basement? Judge Bollinger had not named them, but Mr. Hurlbut thought they were Tiffany, Harrison, the curator Pratt, Dr. Farquharson, and others. He replied that he had never been acquainted with any of them. According to local tradition, Charles Putnam was not part of the old gang. It was reported that he was aloof. "It was his money and he always thought he was a little bit better than the rest of them."[6]

In reply to my question about Reverend Gass, Hurlbut said he knew no specific stories except that "he went off and bought some pottery and brought it back to the museum, and tried to tell people he had dug it up himself." He allegedly bought it in Florida and Arkansas, and Hurlbut said he had seen the collection stored at the museum. Reverend Blumer had the same reputation as Jacob Gass, and no one believed anything he said.

I had heard that some Masonic symbols occurred on the Hunting Scene tablet, but I could not get any confirmation of this from Mr. Hurlbut, who was a Mason. The account that Judge Bollinger told Bailey and Hurlbut was unclear about the sequence of the frauds. Tablets had been planted in the Cook Farm mounds in both 1877 and 1878. Five other tablets came from Cleona township west of Davenport, and at least one more had been "discovered" at Sterling, Illinois. There was a major discrepancy in the narrative that lumped these events together into a single foray. Irving Hurlbut could not recall the judge having spoken about other inscribed-tablet expeditions, and he could not add further details himself.

More information came out when I asked about the elephant pipes. Mr. Hurlbut remembered: "Judge Bollinger said that there was one of the pipes that a farmer had smoked for years, and one of the Academy members dropped and broke it, so they bought it anyhow. The Judge said this and the partridge [pipe from Toolesboro near the mouth of the Iowa River] were genuine." The judge had been ignorant of the fact that the first elephant pipe was a fraud. He had been correct in calling the partridge pipe genuine (figure A.2a).

Obviously, there had been a number of frauds planted, and different individuals were involved. Tiffany, however, had known that the first elephant was a fake.

The second elephant pipe was more generally known to be a hoax. Mr. Hurlbut remembered the judge saying: "There was such a fit made over the first elephant, how there never was an elephant found around there, and they went and made another elephant and a lot of other things. They made them out of softer material that they could carve easily."[7]

In my discussions with Mr. Hurlbut, I became convinced that he was a reliable witness. He made an effort to distinguish between the judge's account and information he had obtained from other sources over the years. He had told his version to many people around the Davenport area, and I was not dredging up remembrances that had not been in his mind. It was an old traditional account and not a new one. Inevitably, an oral tradition is not as accurate as a written account, for alterations in the telling of a story can occur. In the main, I was satisfied that Mr. Hurlbut had accurately presented the case as he had heard it.

Yet, as I reread the transcript many times, I was troubled by some of the details. Not only were there problems with the "genuineness" of the first elephant and the chronology of the fraudulent tablets, but there were other difficulties as well. Making the tablets in the basement of the Academy did not fit with other facts I had learned.

What concerned me the most about the transcript was the form of narration. Hurlbut was unshakable about the story. Judge Bollinger definitely told Bailey and Hurlbut that he had been an active participant. The judge was a crony of the old gang and had personally obtained the slate. I asked, "Can you explain why Judge Bollinger did not become a member of the Academy until 1887?" His reply was simply "I have no idea."[8]

15

THE JUDGE IN THE FIRST PERSON

My doubts about the narrative told by Judge Bollinger began with his date of birth. James Wills Bollinger was born in 1867 in Geneseo, Illinois, the same town where Reverend Adolph Blumer served as a Lutheran minister some years later (figure 15.1). Bollinger's family moved to Davenport in 1873, and James Bollinger was only nine years old in the fall of 1876 when the slate tablets were placed in Mound 3 before the frost hardened the ground. Furthermore, the cornerstone of the Davenport Academy was not laid until 1877, months after the slate tablets were found. The building was not dedicated and occupied until 1878—more than a month after the limestone tablet was found in another Cook Farm mound. We need not waste time speculating whether a boy of nine was drinking with the "old gang" in the basement of a nonexistent building. If the tablets were made by members of the Academy, their activities were carried out in the Odd Fellows Hall. Before the new building was completed, the Davenport Academy rented back rooms from the Odd Fellows for meetings and specimen storage.[1] While it is possible that a group of men might send an interested boy on an errand to get some old slates for the hoax, one would presume that the boy would know where the tablets were carved. Whatever the judge may have said, it appears that he was nowhere near the scene of the events he so vividly described to his entranced audience. His story has the earmarks of a secondhand tale, making Hurlbut's transcript a thirdhand account. This does not deny some

15.1. *Judge James Wills Bollinger (1867–1951). Narrator of the Old Slate House story, Bollinger was a prominent Davenport attorney and businessman and served as president of the museum board, successor to the Academy. (University of Iowa Library, Special Collections)*

basic truth to the story, but it does emphasize the need for caution in accepting its explanation of the events.

Judge Bollinger marred the case by exaggerations and by failing to write down a factual summary. Many parts of his story are confirmed by documents and manuscripts, sources of information that I presume were unknown to him. If he had read them, his narrative would have been more coherent and consistent with the facts. On the other hand, the narrative ascribed to him contains unsubstantiated but plausible explanations more difficult to verify. Within this group of problematic details are the sources for the slate and limestone tablets, the manufacture of the second elephant in the basement, the role and behavior of Reverend Gass in the affair, and the extent to which Academy members were involved in the frauds. However, Dr. Lindley's testimony hints at similar explanations; and Pratt's denials about oil-soaked pipes, the Tiffany quartz crystal, and Schmidt's Quarry show that most of the judge's stories

were current at the time of the controversy. Where, then, did the
judge get his information?

In 1885 Bollinger graduated from Davenport High School, and
he did not join the Davenport Academy until 1887, a decade after
the tablets were found but a time when the controversy was a flam-
ing issue among the membership. Dr. Lindley had just made his
unsuccessful comeback by organizing the opposition ticket to Putnam's leadership, and Charles Harrison became president in January 1887 to continue the Putnam faction. Any member, even a
young one, must have heard many stories about the affair. Through
the 1890s, successive Academy presidents stoutly defended the
relics in published speeches, but gossip about the janitor and the
other stories must have been common knowledge among many
members.

At the time Bollinger joined, he was attending the University of
Iowa, and there is no reference to him in the *Proceedings* beyond
the fact of his membership. He was not active in Academy affairs at
this period of his life and was not a resident of the town. After law
school, he returned to Davenport and practiced law, later serving on
the bench of the Seventh Judicial District of the state from 1897 to
1911. He resigned in that year to go into business, retaining the
courtesy title of judge. Prominent and successful, he was president
of the State Bar Association in 1909 and later of two Davenport
companies. Among numerous clubs and associations, Bollinger
maintained his membership in the Academy; and after it had developed into the Davenport Museum, he was elected president of the
museum board. Amidst a wide circle of friends, including a number
of men with first- or secondhand information about the affair, the
judge undoubtedly came to know the main outlines of the story.

But why had he told it in the first person? Could there be a
mistake? In the course of sending the transcript back to Mr. Hurlbut
for corrections, I wrote him about the chronological problems. He
replied by letter, insisting that the narrative was essentially correct
in the form in which it stood, and that to the best of his knowledge
and memory, it was the way it had been told to Bailey and himself
some twenty years earlier. He added that John Bailey and he had
discussed it many times. Bailey was of the opinion that retelling the
story would just cause trouble and they had better keep quiet about
it. In the 1950s, there were four different museum directors.
Hurlbut mentioned the matter to each of them, and the first three
advised him to keep quiet about it. The gist of their reasoning was:
"It might give the museum a bad name . . . and no one would believe it now because there were no living witnesses to the occasion."

The fourth director, Donald Herold, was not only interested in the story but followed up the tangled evidence and began to assemble it. It was his efforts that eventually got me interested in the case. The letter from Irving Hurlbut in 1969 concluded, "But this is my story, and it is the truth, and I am going to stick to it, and I don't care if anyone believes me or not."[2]

Judge Bollinger decided to give his outstanding collection of Abraham Lincoln memorabilia and books to the University of Iowa Library, and this decision seems to have been confirmed in writing as early as 1943. At the time the gift was finally made in 1951, shortly after his death, the librarian at the university—the now-retired director of Special Collections, Frank Paluka—wrote that it was among the six most complete and useful collections on Lincoln in the country. There is no reference to the Davenport affair in the collection. The fact of the intended gift is mentioned in the Hurlbut transcript.

The judge might well have been the sort of man to exaggerate or invent his role in the affair to improve a good story. He was widely appreciated among his circle of friends as a gourmet and bon vivant—the judge's favorite recipes were published in 1939 in *Better Homes and Gardens.* More to the point, he was also well known as a raconteur, a storyteller, who was well versed in creating a dramatic effect for his listeners. Furthermore, such a lie was beyond the pale of the law. When I reviewed the transcript, it became apparent that he had carefully avoided mentioning anyone by name except for Gass and Tiffany—both of whom were mentioned in print in connection with the affair. He named no others except himself and so lived up to his reputation as an able lawyer.

As I interpret his narrative, the judge was a craftsman who carefully built up the suspense to create a grand illusion. He began by saying he would die in a few months and now wished to tell the whole truth about the Davenport mystery. He actually lived at least three more years, but the impression of an imminent death gave a compelling tone to the story, a ring of sincerity, the aura of a deathbed confession. The stage setting was perfect, with drinks and a leisurely gourmet meal in a private room. He spoke of various matters and delayed coming to the point until after dinner, building up the expectations of his two listeners. The climax finally came. He unfolded his participation in the most famous relic frauds in nineteenth-century American archaeology. It is small wonder that the legend lived on in the area and was retold many times. The judge made a phony confession, but he fully deserved his reputation as a spellbinder.

16

THE CLERGYMAN EMERGES
FROM THE SHADOWS

The investigation inevitably came back to Reverend Jacob Gass. Was he the "biggest windjammer and liar," as Judge Bollinger allegedly said? Was he instead duped by his colleagues, an innocent victim of pranks, as John Bailey believed? There was a third possibility, that the clergyman had a deeper knowledge of the affair, making fools of his tormentors and turning the situation to his own temporary advantage in order to achieve what he hoped might be the lasting glory associated with his discoveries, despite his own knowledge that they were false.

All early, contemporary sources of information considered the clergyman to be an innocent victim, most aptly summarized by A. S. Tiffany's characterization, "honest but not sharp," in his letter to Cyrus Thomas. In turn, Thomas accepted Tiffany's view for several years, until he was shown the fraudulent relics that Gass had sent to H. C. Stevens in Oregon. This led Thomas to question whether the clergyman was "straight," a comment appearing in unpublished correspondence (which affected the way the matter was handled in publications).

Another flaw in the cover story of innocence was the admission by Jacob Gass that his defense in *Science* was manufactured at the Academy, recopied in German, and sent back for "translation." During this process, he wrote a letter to William Pratt, dated 13 April 1886, which not only gave evidence of collusion but, more damaging, mentioned his humiliation at being victimized. The passage in this personal letter is crucial to understanding the affair. It begins with a reference to the correspondence published by A. F. Berlin in the *American Antiquarian* that described his mail-order relic business and concludes with broader implications of impostures that victimized the clergyman: "Oh, it has been such a dreadful carelessness in me to let such letters be written and sent away without examining the contents, and I must now suffer severely enough for this carelessness. Oh when will this storm be past and peace restored, for which I long so much!—Of late I have often thought how happy are the dead, whose rest cannot be disturbed, compared with such an unfortunate being as I am, who has been the victim of all."[1]

This personal note, originally written in German, was translated into English because Gass could not correspond directly in that language. Charles Putnam's defense of Gass, published in *Science* under Gass's name, had the clergyman declare he had no knowledge of frauds.[2] One part of the Davenport conspiracy was thus the deliberate suppression of the truth about the frauds by Putnam, when he was the Academy president, by the curator, and by the clergyman, who all conspired together to cover up the scandal.

The "victim of all" certainly realized that frauds had been perpetrated on him by 1886, but did he know about it earlier? I suspect that he already knew it by the early 1880s, and indeed this is the explanation for his sudden departure from Davenport in 1883 to reestablish himself in northern Iowa. It may be that Putnam, and possibly Pratt, encouraged him to leave, but there is no documentary evidence on this point.

The museum archives contained a wealth of material about some of the members, including photographs of many of them. There was no file on Reverend Gass, however, an amazing omission when one considers his prominent discoveries and the fact that he was actually employed to conduct research on a part-time basis after the tablets were found. Someone had pruned the files.

In 1969 I learned from J. N. Young that descendants of Reverend Gass still lived in Postville, and we visited with his son and daughter. The son, the late Mr. Arthur Gass, was 84 years old and in poor health. He said that his father had talked about the affair, knew he had been tricked, and did mention the name of "someone who was jealous of him" who had been part of the hoax. Arthur Gass could not remember the name of the man, nor could he recognize it among the names of Academy members I mentioned to him.

Question: Did he say anything about the elephant pipe?
(Showing a picture of it owned by the Gass family.)
Reply: . . . Just that they had made things and buried them
and he dug them up.
Question: Do you recall that he said anything about this? (A
picture of the slate tablet. The picture was owned by the Gass
family.)
Reply: No . . . just that they dug down by the river in the
mounds by Muscatine. . . .
Question: Did he ever talk about the pipes or tablets? Was
anything said about them being planted?
Reply: Not the tablets, he never mentioned those, just
spearheads, arrowheads, stuff like that.[3]

The daughter of Jacob Gass, the late Hertha Gass Erbe, said
that her father talked about the events at Davenport, but not a great
deal, and he knew he had been "fooled."[4] These interviews with the
two children of the clergyman took place in the family home built
by Jacob Gass. There were two pictures of the famous Davenport
relics but no artifact collection. He had rid himself of it years before
his death in 1925.

Jacob Gass originally believed that his tablet discoveries were
genuine, and his enthusiasm quickened after finding them. Duncan
Putnam, secretary of the Academy, wrote in 1880 that although
mounds are very numerous, "not one in ten contains anything of
value." This, he added, does not discourage Mr. Gass. "After opening, say, twenty or more mounds without result, he will commence
the next with as much vigor as the first."[5] The statement about the
number of mounds is no exaggeration. In a brief published note,
Gass reported with disappointment the few artifacts obtained in
1879–80, although seventy-five mounds were explored under his
direction in little more than a year's time.[6] There are no records, but
he seems to have been virtually a full-time employee supported by
the money provided by Charles Putnam. The extent of mound pillaging, for such rapid digging can be dignified by no better term, is
astonishing. That no one questioned such destruction is sympto-
matic of the period. Artifacts, not information, was the goal of the
mound explorers and the institutions that supported them. Yet his
work was dedicated to Academy interests, and early collections in
archaeology at the museum today are largely due to his efforts. He
sold his specimens to the Academy.

It was in the same years following the discovery of the limestone tablet that he began to sell frauds to other collectors; and, in

turn, fraudulent artifacts—the two elephant pipes and other plat-form pipes—were slipped into his excavations or sold to him to add to the Academy's collections. This involvement with bogus speci-mens and the sale of specimens was a turning point in the scandal that Academy officers later struggled to suppress.

Was there anything in the clergyman's later career, any hint of forgery or perjury, which might shed light on his involvement with fake artifacts? I discussed the matter with a resident of Postville, Mr. Stan Schroeder, a local historian, who owned copies of the *Postville Herald* from the 1890s. He sent me typewritten copies of excerpts that provide an interesting sidelight on the central figure of the con-troversy.[7]

Jacob Gass left Davenport at the age of forty, in 1883, to take the pulpit of St. John's Lutheran Church in Postville. He had an active and successful ministry for a decade and organized the con-struction of a large new church in 1890. In 1892, Gass resigned the pastorate, but his congregation refused to accept the resignation. At this point he began to have financial troubles, which became a scan-dal.

He founded the *Iowa Volksblatt,* written in German to compete with the two English-language newspapers in town. In those days, newspapers were cheap to run and went in and out of business continually in small towns. The newspaper apparently lost money, because German-speaking immigrants were learning English and severing ethnic ties. As an example, there were complaints that Gass preached only in German, and English services were needed. The newspaper was a liability; an added problem was a leasing speculation that failed. He and an associate were successfully sued for three hundred dollars, and Gass in turn began a libel suit against the editor of the rival newspaper over the published reports and other remarks that had appeared about the matter. By the end of the year, his congregation voted to release him from the pastorate, and the Lutheran church at Cresco, Iowa, unanimously invited him. He declined, left the ministry in 1894, sold his interest in the *Volksblatt,* and bought a farm at the southern edge of town.

In 1896 a furor arose over a promissory note for five hundred dollars, dated 1894. Gass testified that an insurance man, Mr. A. P. Hale, had forged his name on it. Hale was indicted, arrested in Du-buque, and brought to Waukon. Hale, *protesting his innocence, spent five months in jail awaiting trial,* since he was financially unable to post bond. It was a strange affair because Gass apparently attempted to flee rather than face Hale at the trial date. As the *Post-*

ville Herald reported it: "When his case was called, the complaining witness Gass was conspicuous by his absence. He recently returned to Postville and Hale having received information that he was about to take his departure for Germany for an indefinite sojourn, swore out papers for his arrest."[8]

Jacob Gass was put in jail in his turn, and it was said he deserved it. His trial caused a great commotion, as described by a reporter for the *Postville Herald:* "The big Rev. Gass trial is on at the county seat at Waukon this week, and lawyers and ever so many of our citizens are in attendance as advisors and witnesses."[9]

Charged with perjury, Gass was released on bond. The grand jury, meeting in 1896, did not indict him. A rehearing was, however, scheduled over the previous civil suit. At the earlier trial, Hale, found guilty of forgery, was made responsible for payment of the five-hundred-dollar note. In 1897 the case came to trial again. The lawyers defending Gass had a difficult time because of the general feeling that the former clergyman was a liar and had caused Hale to be falsely imprisoned for months, as well as defrauding him of the money. The lawyers hired by Gass "had to fight the most prominent attorneys in the county . . . and what was equally bad, the united prejudice of the Waukon people and very largely the people of the entire county."[10] The jury deliberated a day and a night. At 4:00 A.M. the next morning, they reached the decision that Gass was innocent.

Hale became desperate—the victim of jury trials, imprisonment, and financial losses. He was charged with embezzling one hundred dollars from an insurance company in Dubuque, where he had tried to make a fresh start. He left unpaid bills behind him during his dramatic escape, and reaching Omaha, committed suicide by taking an overdose of patent medicine shortly before he was due to be apprehended. The newspaper editor in Postville reported Hale's death in 1897 with the comment, "Thus ends the career of a somewhat notorious character in these parts."[11]

In contrast to the man he destroyed, Gass prospered in farming and retired in 1910, building a large wooden home near the Lutheran church that had once been the edge of his farm. The Davenport affair had so disillusioned him that he gave up archaeology and developed an interest in geology as a hobby. He died in 1925.

The former clergyman had been charged with forgery and perjury in his archaeological dealings with relic hunters, and knowingly or innocently, he had purchased frauds for the Academy's collections. When he learned he was "the victim of all," he made no attempt to clear the air and straighten out the mess that had come to surround him. Instead, he let others manufacture the defense published in *Science,* which attempted to mask his dealings in artifacts. Incredibly enough, at the very time he admitted the falsity of the artifacts to Pratt and Putnam, they in turn had combined with others to expel Lindley and Tiffany for saying the same thing—the relics were false.

It is astonishing to learn that Jacob Gass was caught up in a web of forgery and perjury a second time, and within a decade of the Davenport conspiracy. The singular repetition of charges for fraud in artifacts and later civil actions could not be mentioned in a court of law as prejudicial evidence. Scientific inquiries sometimes have different rules of evidence than the contemporary courts; as one illustration, the notorious Piltdown forgery of human paleontological remains led investigators many years later to look into the career of the deceased leading suspect, Charles Dawson, who was always present when others made fabulous discoveries. It seemed relevant to unraveling the tale that Dawson, a solicitor by profession, had been involved in other, earlier frauds and even plagiarism; he was known locally as the "Sussex Wizard." In the case of Reverend Jacob Gass, was the repetition of alleged forgery and perjury a singular coincidence, or did it represent a personality flaw?

In reviewing the brief translated notes appearing at intervals in the Academy *Proceedings,* one is struck by the fact that the clergyman never once claimed that the specimens he found were genuine. On the other hand, his family still had the framed pictures of the slate tablet and the second elephant pipe, but not any representation of the very obviously recent limestone tablet and various platform pipes that Gass had acquired. Both pictures were saved when all else was discarded, accompanied by comments to his children that people put things in mounds and he "dug them up." Still, the pieces of the puzzle did not quite fit. He must have known the truth about the limestone tablet and the fraudulent nature of the specimens he was selling to other collectors. On the other hand, he must have believed in the genuineness of the slates and the elephant pipe throughout his later life, or those pictures would have been torn out of their frames and thrown away. If this reasoning is correct, he never caught on to the full extent of the jokes played against him. But if this was true, why then, in 1886, did he write Pratt the letter complaining that he was the "victim of all?" What lay behind that phrase? The answer lay in restudying the strange and wonderful collection of platform pipes obtained by the clergyman from his two brothers, or excavated while they were with him. He had a low opinion of the Yankee mound diggers and the tricks they played, but the mortal wound came with the dawning recognition that his brother-in-law, Adolph Blumer, might have played him false with the elephant pipes, and the more certain knowledge that his own brother, Edwin Gass, had also destroyed him with forgeries.

17

THE EXTENT OF CONSPIRACY

The Davenport conspiracy may well have begun as a sim-
pleminded prank created in the Academy rooms in the Odd Fellows
Hall. It is not unlikely that the two slate tablets and the limestone
tablet were carved in these temporary quarters by members of the
"old gang." Thereafter the amateur mound explorations soon de-
generated into a confusing maze of tricks, subplots, and chicanery.
The web of artifact hoaxes and frauds quickly stimulated a local
antiquities market, which put a monetary value on artifacts. This
market, in turn, encouraged others to make money by selling
frauds to the Academy, which purchased specimens of all sorts—
good, bad, and indifferent. None of this activity would have influenced the professional study of archaeology during the 1880s
and 1890s had the facts become known to all. Unfortunately, those
who had some knowledge, such as Charles Putnam, decided that
the reputation of the Academy came before the truth, and this laid
the basis of the conspiracy to silence critics and distort the scientific
evidence. Pranks and hoaxes are deplorable but by themselves do
not constitute conspiracy. The unfortunate affair did not become a
conspiracy until Putnam published his legalistic broadsides against
the Smithsonian in 1885 and 1886, accompanied by the removal of
dissident members from the Academy.
In typical detective fiction, the seemingly innocent man often
turns out to be guilty, and suspicious characters are proven innocent of any involvement. In the Davenport cast of characters, there
can be no such last-chapter reversals because everyone has some

connection to the fraudulent artifacts. The guilty butler of English country-house mysteries has his real-life counterpart in the janitor whose wife, Rachel, was his accessory after-the-fact in the Tiffany and Lindley hearings. However, a better analogy in fiction is Agatha Christie's *Murder on the Oriental Express,* where the passengers combine to conceal a crime.

Here is a summary of the chief characters of the Davenport drama:

Reverend Jacob Gass looted mounds in the name of science, and his boastful manner made many personal enemies both inside and outside the Academy. His broken English, spoken in a thick German accent, made him the obvious butt of ethnic jokes among the Yankees. Yet there was more to his personality than abrasive mannerisms, for charges of double-dealings and fraud surrounded him like a cloud, much of it substantiated in Davenport and subsequently in Postville.

Reverend Edwin Gass, the younger brother of Jacob Gass, assisted in some excavations and sold the Academy fifteen fraudulent platform pipes. Not a single genuine specimen is associated with his name in the catalog. A clergyman without a parish in Postville, he reportedly became a saloon keeper until his return to Switzerland.

Reverend Adolph Blumer, brother-in-law of Edwin and Jacob Gass and probable Swiss immigrant, became a suspect in planting the second elephant pipe in the mound, where he "discovered" it with Jacob present. He appears to be associated with at least one other fraudulent-pipe discovery.

Charles E. Harrison, known among friends as the "stonecutter," boasted of his skills in making hieroglyphic tablets and arrowheads. His threats of libel kept Tiffany from telling the investigating committee about the full extent of the frauds. The election of Harrison to the presidency of the Academy touched off an opposition ticket in 1887 by friends of Dr. Lindley and Tiffany, who knew about his involvement with fraudulent artifacts.

John Graham, Academy janitor, made copies of stone pipes in his basement workroom and assisted other members in the manufacture of artifacts for personal collections. He seemingly put fraudulent pipes in the mounds for Jacob Gass to find. The second elephant pipe was alleged to be his work, and the janitor was fully implicated in the scandal.

Dr. Clarence T. Lindley practiced medicine in the Academy's basement in the late 1870s before establishing offices elsewhere, and he witnessed, and perhaps participated in, the artifact hoaxes perpetrated upon Reverend Jacob Gass. An amateur relic collector who stored his collection in the basement, Dr. Lindley boasted he could chip flint and sometimes was said to "improve" the specimens he found. His attempt to defend Tiffany and expose the tablet and pipe frauds led to his own expulsion from Academy membership in 1886. The curator, William Pratt, subsequently accused him of defrauding the government by claiming the value of his artifact collection—destroyed by fire in the state orphanage—to be three thousand dollars.

A. S. Tiffany, poorly educated and an amateur archaeologist, was one of the three founders of the Davenport Academy. He was publicly expelled for writing a letter stating that the elephant pipes were fakes and implying that Harrison had planted the limestone tablet. He privately told friends that the quartz crystal found with the limestone tablet had been borrowed for that purpose from his personal mineral collection. According to oral tradition, his wife gave it to the pranksters while he was out of town. This crystal story was mentioned in the hearings but not resolved.

William H. Pratt ran a business college and served a term as Academy president, later serving as the paid curator. He helped Putnam defend Reverend Gass and the various fraudulent artifacts against attacks from the Smithsonian Institution staff and local members. He also aided Putnam in the cover-up of evidence that Gass knowingly bought and sole fraudulent artifacts. Lindley's claims that Pratt knew all about the Academy-basement frauds are probably true. Dr. Lindley also attempted to demonstrate that Pratt had symptoms of mental instability.

Charles E. Putnam, wealthy benefactor whose fortune came from his legal practice and real-estate investments, threatened to sue anyone who publicly doubted the genuineness of the tablets and other artifacts. With money no object, he hired investigators to gather personal evidence "and make trouble" for detractors of the specimens, in such places as Washington, D.C., Pennsylvania, Wisconsin, and Oregon. As more information about the frauds became available, he nevertheless continued to press his attacks in print and built cover stories to protect Reverend Gass and the Academy from public exposure.

Judge James Bollinger, prominent Davenport attorney and businessman, made a confession to two trusted friends in 1947 that he had obtained the slate from the Old Slate House and helped make the frauds in the Academy basement. The judge put a good story ahead of the truth because the Academy building was not yet built when the slates were carved up, and he himself was only nine years old—too young to be part of the old gang. Although much of the confession parallels the written testimony, other specific details are unique to the account, and it appears that the judge based his confession upon hearsay and the oral tradition he came to know from his later involvement with the Davenport Museum.

As for the conspiracy itself, the origins lay in the clubhouse atmosphere of the Academy, which was still meeting in rooms hired at the Odd Fellows Hall when the slate tablets were buried in one of the Cook Farm mounds nearby. The Yankee gag played upon the braggart Swiss preacher misfired because Gass did not recognize the Old Slate House slates as a source of origin. The slate affair was not a serious hoax concerned with the Mound Builders because there was no attempt to remove the slate holes in the Calendar stone, a dead giveaway. With all of the publicity, the jokers were ashamed to publicly confess, and so they tried to end the affair with an even more obvious fraud—the limestone tablet with Tiffany's crystal, which Gass himself had admired on some prior occasion. To their amazement, the limestone tablet was also accepted as genuine. Growing desperate, the pranksters made further tablets to expose the affair, and Gass found five of them in Cleona township. The sudden disappearance of these tablets and records, together with the lack of publicity, strongly suggests these tablets were almost immediately recognized as frauds. The matter seems to have been hushed up because it cast such serious doubts upon the much-publicized slate and limestone tablets. The conspiracy was beginning, and it was by now beyond the reach of the original jokers.

Meanwhile, an antiquities market was booming in the Davenport area. Reverend Gass himself took advantage of his personal publicity to enter into correspondence with collectors around the country and sell obvious frauds. The janitor, John Graham, and his friends had meanwhile entered into an innocent amusement, making copies of Hopewell pipes for their own use. Graham openly admitted it, and his workbench, tools, and oil used for aging specimens all are mentioned in the testimony. By now, some of these copies had entered into the local antiquities market. More serious, there is an implication that the janitor was one of those putting fake pipes in the burial mounds. As general handyman, Graham assisted Reverend Gass by locating appropriate mounds for excavation. On at least some occasions, Graham visited mound sites months before frauds were excavated from them by the clergyman. This curious cycle of the janitor's mound visits occurred during 1880–82, when the clergyman was working for the Academy on an almost full-time basis. No frauds were found by any Academy member after Gass was seemingly encouraged to leave town before Henry Henshaw's article appeared in the 1884 *Annual Report* of the Bureau of Ethnology. Before Gass left town, his own brother, Edwin Gass, became involved in the antiquities market and sold other frauds to the Academy, using his brother's sponsorship to explain their origin.

Hushing up the frauds led to the formation of the conspiracy. However, there was reason for many members to doubt Dr. Lindley's testimony, which exaggerated the extent of involvement by Academy members. Platform pipes rarely occur in the mounds, but based upon specimen analysis, genuine specimens were found by Tiffany, Lindley, French, Hall, Schmidt, Harrison, Pratt, and Parsons. Although called "stonecutter," Harrison's name is associated with the gifts of five genuine pipes and no frauds; Gass added fifteen genuine pipes to the collections. The absence of fraudulent artifacts explains the shock caused by Lindley's charges that the general membership knew about, or engaged in, the manufacture of fraudulent artifacts and copies. Most members realized that such general charges were simply not true; and indeed, only a small group was involved, including some outside the Academy. At the time of the 1886 hearings, Gass was safely out of town, and no frauds had been added to the Academy collections for some four years. Through ignorance of the facts, the membership expelled its two dissident members, but this was merely a temporary victory because gossip spread the news and by January 1887 the opposition ticket to the Putnam faction had gained thirty votes from new and old members in support of Tiffany and Lindley.

And so the Davenport case for a mysterious, exotic origin for the ancient Mound Builders collapsed amid a welter of claims and countercharges. Cyrus Thomas of the Bureau of Ethnology won the professional case that ancient America had been settled by American Indians. Professionalism put an end to the Mound Builder hoaxes in the late 1880s and early 1890s, and, it seemed, ended the gross speculations that had arisen during the age of mound looting and general antiquarian destruction.

18

AGAIN THE
WANDERING NATIONS

Professor Barry Fell holds distinguished academic credentials in marine biology and invertebrate paleontology and had a professorship at Harvard University, where he is now emeritus. In later years, his career interests in research shifted to linguistics, in which he had no formal training, and he created 'a sensation with his unorthodox conclusions about ancient migrations to America from European and Mediterranean lands. His first book on this subject, *America B.C.*, was written for the public rather than a scholarly audience, and it soon attracted a large layman following. As one indication of its success, the American Booksellers Association presented it to the White House library as one of the 250 best books published in the United States during 1973–77. He subsequently wrote two sequels, in which he sketched out his linguistic evidence of numerous Old World nations that had reached the New World before Columbus.[1]

This chapter is redrafted from my professional publications, including "The Davenport Conspiracy: A Hoax Unravelled," *Early Man* 1 (1979):9–12; "The North American Periphery of Antique Vermont," *Antiquity* 53 (1979):121–23; "Review of *Saga America*, by Barry Fell," *Antiquity* 54 (1980):354–55; "Review of *Saga America*, by Barry Fell," *Archaeology* 34, no. 1 (1981): 62–66; "Prehistoric Vermont and the Antiquarian Revolt," *Vermont History* 28 (1980):183–87; "Canaanites in America: A New Scripture in Stone?" *Biblical Archaeologist* 42 (1979):137–40; "Deciphering Ancient America," *The Skeptical Inquirer* 5, no. 3 (1981):44–50, reprinted in *Science Confronts the Paranormal*, ed. Kendrick Fraizer (Buffalo: Prometheus Press, 1986).

Numerous other amateur-authored books with the theme of foreign invasions of ancient America had appeared over the years, but
these generally had attracted far less attention and notoriety.[2] Professor Fell's books differed from these amateurish attempts because
he was a Harvard professor and his decipherments were so abstruse
that they could not be readily challenged by the reading public. His
linguistic findings generated a minor social movement, a populist
wave of speculation about ancient empires and lost kingdoms
equivalent to the pervasive nineteenth-century speculations about
"civilized" European Mound Builders and "savage" Indians.

Shortly after *America B.C.* appeared, a summary of it was published by the *Reader's Digest* under the provocative title "Who Discovered America?" The answer was Phoenician Canaanites, who
once held sway over half the continent, aided by Egyptians and Old
Celts. The author of this article particularly praised the decipherment of the Cremation Scene slate tablet, terming it an American
equivalent of the Rosetta stone from Egypt, which had unlocked the
mysteries of ancient history.[3] The new ancient history revealed that
Egyptians, along with Libyans and Phoenicians, had explored the
upper Mississippi valley around 800 B.C. and settled in what is now
the Quad Cities, where they camped at the Cook Farm mounds.
Libyan crewmen, therefore, carved the elephant pipes.

Professor Fell published the translation of his decipherment of
the Davenport shingle, which adds the final ludicrous note to the
Davenport conspiracy:

> EGYPTIAN INSCRIPTION: To a pillar attach a mirror in such
> manner that when the sun rises on New Year's Day it will cast a
> reflection on the stone called "The Watcher." New Year's Day
> occurs when the sun is in conjunction with the zodiacal constel-
> lation Aries, in the House of the Ram, the balance of night and
> day being about to reverse. At this time (the spring equinox)
> hold the festival of the New Year and the religious rite of the New
> Year.

> LIBYAN-PHOENICIAN INSCRIPTION: The stone is inscribed
> around with a record . . . ; it reveals the naming, the length, the
> placing of the seasons.

> IBERIC-PHOENICIAN INSCRIPTION: Set out around [this is] a
> secret [secret sign] text defining the season's delimiting.[4]

Professor Fell ignored warnings from Carol Hunt, registrar of
the Putnam Museum, that the slate shingle was a fraud.[5] His

description of the discovery contains errors concerning the identification of the stone and the year it was found, and it also contains
errors in the years and place of discovery of the elephant pipes. His
refusal to discuss or even cite *The Davenport Conspiracy* or the
earlier Smithsonian staff reports indicates his lack of control over
the archaeological context of the specimens; bypassing archaeological studies is a general plague in his book.

In his reconstruction of the foreign travelers to the Quad Cities,
Fell ignored Mediterranean history. There was no Libyan maritime
empire; *Libya* was the term in classical usage for the continent of
Africa. *Phoenician* and *Punic* are the Greek and Roman names for
the Canaanites of present-day Lebanon and their western Mediterranean colonies. The earliest settlements, such as Carthage, had
barely started by 800 B.C., and there were no trading posts in Spain
for another century or two, which makes a Mississippi exploration
in 800 B.C. physically impossible. The Egyptian addition to the exploration in America on "chartered" ships is an impossibility
without the presence of either Libyans or Phoenicians.

The elephant pipes allegedly made by Libyan crewmen add
another dimension to this scenario. One of these pipes clearly represents the Pleistocene woolly mammoth, a forgery copied from well-
known drawings of European mammoths, which were not living in
North Africa in 800 B.C. War elephants were introduced into North
Africa following the conquests of India by Alexander the Great,
some five centuries too late for the Libyan crewmen to have seen
them.

Fell's linguistic decipherment represents another series of com-
pounded errors. The real story is that the forgers scrawled out nonsense, anything to fool Gass, without intending to produce a message. This description exactly matches what one sees scratched into
the Cremation Scene tablet: an inscription made up of Greek letters,
two anachronistic Arabic numbers, Roman letters, recognizable
musical clef symbols, ampersands, scrawls, squares with dots, and
irregular curves (figure 18.1). I have shown this inscription to Jonas
Greenfield, professor of ancient Semitic languages at Hebrew University, and he states that the script letters cannot be Semitic or
Egyptian but represent a clear and recent hoax. Furthermore, Fell
produced far too many words to fit the number of signs; the lengthy
"Egyptian" text is based upon thirty to fifty letters, and the two
briefer "Phoenician" texts on nineteen and twenty letters.

Turning to a wider view of the problems raised by Professor
Fell's linguistic theories, it must be stated that the successful de-

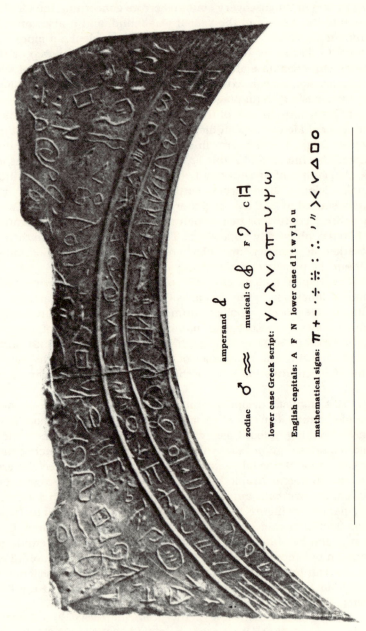

ampersand &

zodiac ♂ ♒   musical: G 𝄢 𝄞 F ♩ c 𝄐

lower case Greek script: γ ζ λ ∨ ο π τ υ ψ ω

English capitals: A F N lower case d l t w y i o u

mathematical signs: π + – · ÷ ≠ ∴ ∵ ′ ″ × ⟨ ◁ □ o

18.1 Modern symbols inscribed on the Cremation Scene tablet. Fell's false decipherment appears on page 148. See also figure 2.7. (Putnam Museum specimen AR-15338) cipherment of a text depends upon the correct identification of the alphabet or other writing system used. Where these symbols are phonetic in value, as in alphabetic or syllabic scripts, the pronunciation or transliteration of the words identifies the language. While this is a simplification of the complexities involved in a true decipherment of a previously unread script, it does represent a fundamental necessity. When the script is incorrectly identified, there is *no chance* for valid decipherment. Examinations of the scripts allegedly deciphered by Professor Fell show them to be illusional and in various ways misidentified—criticisms that lie at the heart of the rejection of his work.

As one example of script misidentification, Professor Fell sees Libyan and Egyptian characters upon a specimen named the Long Island tablet. In contrast, anthropologists—beginning with Daniel Brinton in 1893—identify the symbols as typical aboriginal petroglyphs, which include a bow and arrow, a man and a canoe, a possible wigwam, a bird, a deer, a fish, an eel, and a bear's paw. No citation to the anthropological literature on this tablet appears in Professor Fell's book, which must lead many of the general public to assume that none exists. Fell transforms the aboriginal canoe into a Libyan galley and translates the native petroglyphs to read, "This ship is a vessel from the Egyptian Dominions."[6] I have been told by a credible source that this petroglyphic tablet was a fraud, manufactured in the 1890s by a student as part of a joke played on his professor, Brinton.

A closer parallel to the Davenport decipherment is Professor Fell's interpretation of the Grave Creek tablet. That well-known hoax was perpetrated in the 1830s to add an attraction to the private museum at the Grave Creek mound diggings in what is now West Virginia. Testimony from workmen in later years demonstrated that the Grave Creek tablet turned up without any association with the excavations. Its short inscription is a mixture of letters from different alphabets, without any known intent to be decipherable, and all of this information about the fraud has been available since 1894, when it was published by Cyrus Thomas in one of the most important reports on nineteenth-century American archaeology.[7] Without any hint to his readers about this archaeological context, Professor Fell deciphers the Grave Creek tablet as if it were a legitimate inscription and says it reads, "The memorial of Teth. This tile [his] brother caused to be made."[8]

Other choices of American inscriptions prove equally unfortunate. Professor Fell identifies a Roman numeral for thirty, XXX, as

part of a "Celtic calendar" on the Beltane Stone at the Mystery Hill
site in New Hampshire. The stone was reexamined by professors
Charles Cazeau and Stuart Scott, a geologist and an anthropologist
respectively, and they found that the unmodified granite veins had
been misidentified as Helios markings.[9]

Other decipherments are merely ludicrous. For instance, the
Bourne Stone from Massachusetts has markings of unknown recent
origin, yet Fell deciphered them to read that the Massachusetts ter-
ritory had been annexed into the Carthaginian Empire by a General
Hanno: "A Proclamation of Annexation. Do not deface. By this
Hanno takes possession."[10] The Carthaginians are not known to
have ever sailed west from their trading post in Morocco, Lixus, but
every known inscription from the Mediterranean is written in the
Phoenician alphabet. This Massachusetts stone purports to show us
with its stray marks that a mystery ship arrived with a phantom
crew who lost their letters along the way.

America B.C. also furthered controversy over the Old Irish
script, ogham, which Professor Fell claimed exists in American inscriptions. Irish ogham developed after the fourth century A.D. as a
writing system using groups of linear marks to represent fifteen
consonants and groups of dots for five vowels. Although this inno-
vative script developed separately from traditional European alpha-
betical characters, each of the ogham letters derives its phonetic
values from written Latin of the late Roman empire. Ogham script
had a very restricted range in eastern Ireland and adjacent colonies
across the Irish Sea in Wales and Scotland; moreover, it was only
used for brief funerary commemorations, sometimes accompanied
by a parallel Latin inscription. The furor over Professor Fell's
claimed decipherments of what we should call "American ogham"
came about because he made the following claims: (1) Phoenicians
learned ogham from the Irish; (2) they wrote it entirely in consonants, without vowels; (3) the Irish in turn learned from the Phoenicians to write what we will term "American Gaelic," without vowels; (4) meanwhile, Celtic tribes all the way south into Spain were
writing in ogham, which no one had known until Professor Fell said
it was so; (5) all of this ogham in North America and western Europe
took the form of casual scratch marks, in contrast to the rigid rules
governing ogham writing as it was actually known in Ireland; and
finally, (6) ogham writing dated back a thousand years or more earlier than its first known occurrence during the period of the late
Roman Empire.

Readers thinking that my discussion has become unexpectedly

garbled need not blame the typesetter, for I have merely presented the totally unsupported and speculative reasoning that lay behind a massive series of New England decipherments that created a very considerable commotion. As an example, Professor Fell viewed three more or less straight lines of unknown origin on a rock at Mystery Hill, which he deciphered using his own methods. The three lines became a *BL* under the American variation of the Irish rules, and since Fell thought that vowels were unimportant or not written, he added vowels of his choosing, the *AA* dipthong, between the consonants. From this perception, the three lines emerged as the word *BAAL*, and Mystery Hill conjured up specters of ancient Canaanite-Phoenicians raising this mighty altar to their great god Baal. Amateur enthusiasts from all over New England began to send Professor Fell drawings of lines they encountered on stones, and he deciphered them all as ancient Celtic and Phoenician ogham inscriptions. Mystery Hill became known as an America's Stonehenge, and by my first visit, the New Hampshire Tourist Information Center had distributed brochures and had put up a state sign pointing the way to New Hampshire's own Phoenician ceremonial shrine.

The antiquarian excitement brought international attention to these discoveries. Professor Glyn Daniel of Cambridge University visited the sites, scoffed, and wrote a stinging review of *America B.C.* in the *New York Times Sunday Review of Books*, which brought a flood of irate letters written by believers in the mystery script.

Two specialists in archaeology and in real Irish ogham came over from the British Isles to attend the Castleton Conference in Vermont, where antiquarians outnumbered the archaeologists in the wrangle over old coins, shrines, and ogham. Anne Ross and Peter Reynolds reviewed their findings in the English journal *Antiquity* in 1978. They identified the American ogham at Vermont's Crow site as plow marks on an exposed field boulder, the marks running parallel to the old stone walls on the abandoned nineteenth-century farmstead. They demonstrated conclusively that the plow marks had been made on the stone by a horse-drawn, single-share plow similar to the Gloucestershire type formerly used in small-field cultivation in England. Other examples of American ogham they reported to be, variously, natural striations, glacial scratches, or marks of recent origin. None of it resembled genuine Irish ogham script.[11]

Professor Fell had been very eclectic in his choice of scripts to

decipher, and one of his claims was the survival of Egyptian
hieroglyphic script among the Algonkian Micmac Indians of
Canada. This claim and others were rejected in a summary review
in 1978 by two staff anthropologists at the Smithsonian Institution,
Ives Goddard and William Fitzhugh.[12]

Professor Fell stated that various Old World and native American languages were closely related, if not the same language, and he
termed these "interface tongues," naming among them Libyan-
Zuni, Iberic-Pima, and others. In his 1980 book, *Saga America*, and
in other writings, he added Basque-Susquehanna, Celtic-Algonkian,
Greek-Libyan-Algonkian, and other mixtures. It must be emphasized here that since the nineteenth century, it has been well known
that native American languages are totally different in grammar,
vocabulary, and origin from European and Mediterranean language
families. From the perspective of anthropological linguistics, the
only question worth pursuing has been the issue of possible "loan
words" representing unrecorded contacts between European and
other Old World peoples with native Americans. There are numerous examples of loan words that passed in both directions during
the post-Columbian colonial period; for example, the English *to-
mato* was introduced indirectly as both plant and word from the
Aztec of Mexico. Technical linguistics is necessary to estimate the
probabilities of a loan word being prehistoric or post-Columbian,
and there remain uncertainties. In summary, research has never
successfully demonstrated that any unequivocal pre-Columbian
loan words were introduced from Europe into native American languages.[13]

One study illustrates that this generality remains true, despite
claims to the contrary. Professor Fell wrote that the Old Irish Celts
named the physical features of New England, and subsequently the
natives adapted these names in their own languages—Al-
gonkianized them, as it were. The New England settlers often used
the native Algonkian place-names, although these were ordinarily
corrupted, abbreviated, or variously misspelled. The question is
whether Algonkian-sounding place-names conceal ancient Celtic
roots. A Celtic-language specialist, Professor William Nicolaisen,
carefully analyzed the Celtic root words in New England Algonkian
place-names that were listed in *America B.C.* He found every example to be spurious.[14] Professor Fell never responded to Nicolaisen,
but he later proposed in *Saga America* that the native Algonkian
languages were derived from ancient Greek, a dialect that included
Libyan.

Not only have the scripts, languages, and decipherments that formed the basis for Professor Fell's foreign invasions been reevaluated, some of the sites mentioned in his writings have been reexamined as well. The state archaeologist of Vermont, Giovanna Neudorfer, has investigated a series of stone structures in the Green Mountains that antiquarians were naming stonehenges, shrines, and megalithic monuments of antiquity. One of these seems to have been built as the hideout for a crazed Civil War deserter, while others were nineteenth-century Yankee farmsteads or root cellars for turnips fed to sheep when the wool industry flourished.[15]

A Yankee farm artifact of the nineteenth century is a lye stone, a flat rock with a groove around the perimeter. Ashes on the stone had water poured over them, forming lye, which ran from the channel into a barrel; lye mixed with tallow made strong, soft soap, which was cheaper than store-bought soap. Just such a lye stone at Mystery Hill is venerated by antiquarian enthusiasts as an altar of human sacrifice (for they imagine blood in the lye grooves), dedicated perhaps to the god Baal, whose name appears nearby. Back in 1939 and 1940, Professor Hugh Hencken of Harvard, a specialist in languages and Irish archaeology, published two articles on Mystery Hill. A retired insurance executive from Hartford had bought the place, thinking it was a twelve-hundred-year-old monastic refuge of Culdee monks from Ireland. Hencken wrote that there was nothing Irish, modern or ancient, in the stone cellars, walls, or other alignments; and in a jovial way, he scoffed at a theory of Irish priests with a sacrificial altar, which he was the first to identify as a Yankee lye stone. He also explained the eccentricity of the stuctures' construction by recounting the New Hampshire tradition that the stone structures were built in the first half of the nineteenth century by a local character, Jonathan Pattee, who by general opinion "had been crazy."[16]

Affairs reached the loony stage. *America B.C.* touched upon the subject of ancient European fertility cults introduced into New England, a place well known for glacial boulders. Fields of boulders and separate, isolated boulders—called "erratics"—now became subjects for fantasy, as Professor Fell and his followers identified the "ball"-stones and "penis"-stones revered by ancient Celtic forebears.

The reading public had other books that confirmed, in a general way, Professor Fell's linguistic theories of massive foreign empires and amazing migrations. An amateur, Salvatore Trento, wrote *The Search for Lost America*, which found Phoenician and European megalithic monuments from sea to shining sea, and incidentally accepted Fell's interpretation of the Davenport slate shingle.[17] *Before Columbus* and *Riddles in History,* by Professor Cyrus Gordon, accepted the evidence of misidentified coins, vintage Viking hoaxes, a well-known Brazilian forgery, and a scrap of 1820s Cherokee syllabary on the Bat Creek tablet from Tennessee, and from all this concocted Hebrew and Canaanite migrations into the Americas.[18] Much of what was being published closely reflected our civilization's enchantment with space fiction, Atlantean supermen, and ghosts of the dead.[19] An illustration of contemporaneity is provided by an African-American professor of black studies at Rutgers, whose book *They Came Before Columbus* added affirmative action to the blooming antiquarianism—his thesis is that black Africans ruled ancient Mesoamerica and that the Phoenicians were merely their servants and not their masters.[20]

Professor Fell published *Saga America* in 1980 as a linguistic interpretation of the post-Egyptian period in pre-Columbian America, and the devastating reviews it received in those archaeological journals that deigned to notice it made little or no impact upon a large and loyal following. The book made incredible claims without any archaeological substance whatever. For Professor Fell, the Davenport shingle remained genuine. Ogham script provided the key to prehistory. Native American petroglyphic rock drawings from the western United States were now transformed into mystery scripts and languages. He added runic letters nominally of northern European origin to his linguistic inventory, and a most startling invention of terminology resulted—Runic-Shawnee, Welsh-Ogham, Greek-Libyan-Algonkian, and Basque-this-and-that. His writing declined into folktale-prehistory as he seemed to search out every forgery and spurious literary tradition and enlarge upon them, creating others out of dubious coins.[21] He perpetuated the myth of Vikings building Newport Cathedral in Rhode Island—in 1350, if a date is required—although archaeological excavations at that small stone tower in the late 1940s had conclusively demonstrated that it was colonial American vintage, built as a lookout by Governor Benedict Arnold of Rhode Island, grandfather of the traitor.[22] There were Minnesota and Oklahoma Vikings. He believed the myth of Prince Madok and traced Welsh-Indian genealogy through petroglyphs in the American Southwest. In Fell's book the Roman Empire reached the New World, Christians later fled across the Atlantic to escape Vandals, Syrians established a naval academy in Nevada and also mapped Hawaii, Iberians established a bank of Wyoming, and Vinland Vikings reverted to paganism. More of the same sort of unsubstantiated linguistic prehistory reappeared in 1982 under the title *Bronze Age America*. But North America had no Bronze Age because it had no bronze; Professor Fell had misunderstood the indigenous Old Copper Culture of the Archaic Period and had attributed it all to foreigners. It is enough to say that he traced the activities of Ontario Vikings more than two thousand years before there were Vikings in Scandinavia and nearly twenty-five hundred years before the Norsemen inhabited Iceland, which led them to Greenland and the discovery of the North American coast.

By this time, Professor Fell was content to become an antiquarian cult figure in San Diego, and as his public influence waned, his die-hard supporters closed ranks around him. The novelty had faded of a retired Harvard professor who transformed prehistoric America into a folk history of Old-World linguistic invasions. It is unlikely that Professor Fell will be forgotten. Although *Saga America* (1980) and *Bronze Age America* (1982) are already out of print, awaiting rediscovery by the next generation of enthusiasts, his first book, *America B.C.*, remains available through a recent reprinting. Terribly wrong books have a way of surviving indefinitely. A garbled book on Lost Atlantis lives after fifty reprintings and remains a primary source for occult belief in the mysterious continent. A book inspiring belief in universal Egyptian civilization, contrary to all archaeological findings, is still alive after eighty years, and an error-strewn defense of the bogus Kensington rune stone of Minnesota still has its readers after fifty years. We may therefore suppose that *America B.C.* will achieve its share of immortality over the next decades.

We have something to learn about our contemporary civilization. Growing enchantment with outer space, science fiction, astrology, eastern mysticism, and other marvels allows an easier acceptance of the more down-to-earth doings of wandering Israelites, Egyptians, and Vikings. A New Antiquarianism must be receiving part of its stimulus from the rising interest in the occult. This is but part of the explanation. There are also racist, or at least ethnic, overtones to contemporary antiquarianism that many find appealing.

A strong ethnocentricity finds its way into claims of ancient migrations; it is manifested in root-finding by a nation of immigrants from different modern lands. Ethnic Scandinavians search for Vikings, Portuguese for earlier explorers, an African-American finds blacks in Mesoamerica, Irish and Welsh descendants have

their myths, the earl of Orkney becomes a Scottish Columbus, a
Jewish scholar reports Canaanite and Hebrew migrations, and the
present ruler of Libya has come to believe in the American Indian's
Libyan heritage. Not all ancestors come from across the Atlantic,
however, and this fact too is reflected in the growing stories about
ancient imperialism. An ethnic Chinese has written two incredible
books on the Chinese-Maya; a gentleman from India writes of the
influence his land had in Central America.

These quaint studies advancing a single ethnic claim have usually enjoyed reasonable sales in the paperback marketplace. However, the rip-roaring publishing successes seem reserved for those
who promote almost every conceivable ethnic claim simulta-
neously, giving something to everyone, and with it the hope that
your neighbor's success advances your own cause. With the climate
of fantasies in contemporary society, and the extent to which these
books reflect those fantasies, we are most likely nearer the beginning than the end of this cycle of derivative archaeological fiction.

THE DAVENPORT PIPES

Table A.1. *Platform pipes formerly in the Davenport Museum*

Old number	Shetrone[a] evaluation	Bowl shape	Provenience	Date	Collector	PDANS[b] reference
2923	Genuine	Plain	Iowa	1917	Paarman	—
2924	Genuine	Bird head	SE Iowa	1914	Michelson	—
4446	Genuine	Plain	Cook farm	1874	Gass	1:117–43
4533	Genuine	Plain	Illinois	1875	French, Tiffany	1:114
4564	Genuine	Plain	SE Iowa	1877	Gass	2:150
4566	Genuine	Plain	Illinois	1877	Hall	3:48
4570	Genuine	Plain	—	—	Hall	—
7060	Genuine	Plain	SE Iowa	1880	Gass[c]	3:143
7389	Genuine	Plain	SE Iowa	1880	Gass[c]	3:145
7390	Genuine	Plain	SE Iowa	1880	Gass[c]	3:143, 145
7391	Genuine	Plain	SE Iowa	1880	Gass[c]	3:143, 145
8287	Genuine	Plain	Wisconsin	1883	Hall	4:233
7061	Fraud	Swain	SE Iowa	1880	Gronen[c]	3:145
7067	Fraud	Plain	Illinois	1880	Gass	3:138 (?)
7388	Fraud	Plain	Illinois	1880	Gass[c]	3:139
7619	Fraud	Serpent	Illinois	1880	Hitt	3:148
8275	Fraud	Plain	Illinois	1883	Ed. Gass[c]	4:222, 233
8280	Fraud	Eagle	Illinois	1883	Ed. Gass[c]	4:222, 233
8281	Fraud	Deer head	Illinois	1883	Ed. Gass[c]	4:222, 233
8284	Fraud	Animal	Illinois	1883	Ed. Gass[c]	4:222, 233
8357	Fraud	Plain	NE Iowa	1880	—	—

[a]Shetrone (1930MSa) evaluation of specimens subsequently missing from the collections.
[b]*Proceedings of the Davenport Academy of Natural Sciences.*
[c]Donor or purchaser not identified as excavator.

Table A.2. Identification of fraudulent pipes in the Davenport Museum

Figure	Bowl	Old number	New number	Date	Area	Collector	PDANS[a] reference
13.1a	Elephant	6782	AR 14778	1880	SE Iowa	Blumer, Gass	3:133
13.1b	Elephant	6355	AR 14779	1878	SE Iowa	Gass[b]	2:348
13.1c	Bear	8282	AR 14377	1883	Illinois	Ed. Gass[b]	4:222, 233
13.2a	Bird	8286	AR 14383	1883	SE Iowa	Ed. Gass[b]	4:233
13.2b	Bird	6783	AR 14497	1880	SE Iowa	Blumer, Gass	3:130, 133
13.2c	Animal	4798	AR 14504	1882	SE Iowa	Gass, Ed. Gass	4:216 (?)
13.3a	Human head	6786	AR 14491	1880	Missouri	Gass[b]	3:108
13.3b	Beaver (?)	7798	AR 14373	1882	SE Iowa	Gass[b]	4:216
13.3c	Beaver (?)	6785	AR 14374	1879	Illinois	Gass	3:137
13.4a	Wolf	7387	AR 14381	1880	Illinois	Gass[b]	3:139
13.4b	Lizard	7546	AR 14376	1880	Illinois	Gass[b]	3:147
13.4c	Turtle	7624	AR 14375	—	Illinois		—
13.5a	Beetle	7547	AR 14486	1880	Illinois	Gass[b]	3:147
13.5b	Fox	8283	AR 14385	1883	Illinois	Ed. Gass[b]	4:222, 233
13.5c	Bird	8278	AR 14372	1883	Illinois	Ed. Gass[b]	4:222, 233
13.5d	Bird	8279	AR 14378	1883	Illinois	Ed. Gass[b]	4:222, 233
13.5e	Bear	6732	AR 14370	—	SE Iowa	Gass	2:348
13.6a	Plain	8273	AR 14499	1883	SE Iowa	Ed. Gass[b]	4:222, 233
13.6b	Plain	8274	AR 14506	1883	SE Iowa	Ed. Gass[b]	4:222, 233
13.6c	Plain	7622	AR 14509	1881	Illinois	Gass	3:186–92
13.6d	Animal	7625	AR 14508	—	Illinois	—	—
13.6e	Plain	8276	AR 14498	1883 (?)	Illinois	Ed. Gass[b]	4:222, 233
13.6f	Plain	7621	AR 14500	1881	Illinois	Gass	3:186–92
13.6g	Plain	8285	AR 14505	1883	SE Iowa	Ed. Gass[b]	4:222, 233
13.6h	Animal	8277	AR 14507	1882 (?)	SE Iowa	Ed. Gass[b]	4:216 (?)

[a]Proceedings of the Davenport Academy of Natural Sciences.
[b]Donor or purchaser not identified as excavator.

161

Table A.3. Identification of genuine pipes in the Davenport Museum

Figure	Bowl	Old number	New number	Date	Area	Collector	PDANS[a] reference
13.7a	Plain	4458	AR 15061	1874	Cook farm	Gass	1:117–43
13.7b	Plain	8360	AR 15027	1886	SE Iowa	Harrison	5:43–44
13.7c	Plain	4461	AR 15064	1874	Cook farm	Gass	1:121
13.7d	Plain	4491	AR 15060	1874	Cook farm	Gass	1:117–43
13.7e	Plain	4466	AR 15058	1874	Cook farm	Gass	1:122
13.7f	Plain	2927	AR 14388	1914	SE Iowa	Michelson	—
13.7g	Blank	4559	AR 15024	1875	SE Iowa	Parsons	1:111
A.1a	Frog	4445	AR 15063	1874	Cook farm	Gass	1:117–43
A.1b	Dog (?)	4490	AR 15065	1874	Cook farm	Gass	1:120
A.1c	Bird	4450	AR 15105	1874	Cook farm	Schmidt	1:120
A.2a	Bird	4562	AR 15025	1875	SE Iowa	Harrison	1:106–11
A.2b	Bird	4563	AR 15026	1875	SE Iowa	Pratt, Harrison	1:106–11
A.2c	Wildcat[b]	4558	AR 15030	1875	SE Iowa	Harrison, Pratt, Parsons	1:79
A.3a	Plain	8359	AR 15028	1886	SE Iowa	Harrison	5:39
A.3b	Plain	9656	AR 15016	1908	Illinois	Nickerson	—
A.3c	Plain	7066	AR 15059	1880	Illinois	Gass[c]	4:18 (?)
A.3d	Plain	7620	AR 14382	1881 (?)	Illinois	Gass	3:187 (?)
A.3e	Plain	7623	AR 15062	—	Illinois	—	—
A.3f	Plain	4565	AR 15057	1875	SE Iowa	Tiffany	1:113

[a]*Proceedings of the Davenport Academy of Natural Sciences.*
[b]Genuineness not certain (McKusick).
[c]Donor or purchaser not identified as excavator.

162

A.1. Genuine effigy platform pipes: (a) *frog,* (b) *dog,* (c) *bird. (Put-nam Museum specimens)*

163

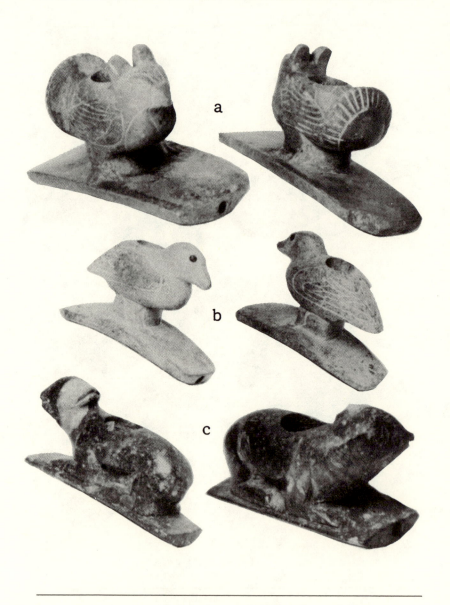

A.2. Genuine effigy platform pipes: (a, b) birds, (c) wildcat. (Putnam Museum specimens)

164

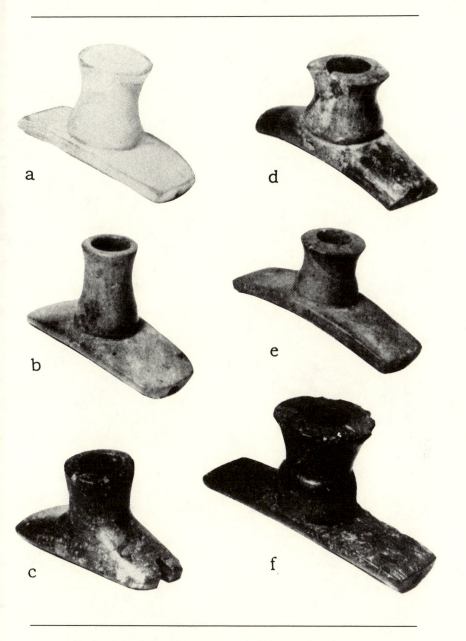

a

d

b

e

c

f

A.3.   Genuine plain platform pipes. (Putnam Museum specimens)

NOTES

CHAPTER 1

1. Willey and Sabloff 1980:15.
2. Ibid. 15-17.
3. Silverberg 1968.
4. Powell 1894.
5. Squire and Davis 1848: 301
6. Snow 1980:31-81.
7. Ibid.
8. Ibid. 51-81.
9. Haven 1855; Willey and Sabloff 1980:35, 39.
10. Schwartz 1967:6-36.
11. Silverberg 1968.
12. Morison 1971:244-47; Godfrey 1955:40.
13. McKusick 1979b; Reid 1878.
14. Thomas 1894; Silverberg 1968:102-6.
15. Farquharson 1877, 1877a, 1879.
16. Harrison 1880.
17. Farquharson 1880:67; Barber 1882:276; Blumer 1882:132-33.
18. Putnam 1886:341.
19. Meltzer and Sturtevant 1983:325-33.
20. Scott County histories from 1910 through the 1930s defended the authenticity of the relics, one measure of local public opinion.

CHAPTER 2

1. Thomas 1894:642.
2. Henshaw 1883:158.
3. Gass, Erbe 1969MS.
4. Putnam 1886MS.
5. Hurlbut 1969MS.
6. Reverend Gass's interest in Swiss archaeology is conjectural and could not be confirmed in my 1969 discussions with his two children.
7. This Cook Farm mound site is now 2040 West River Street (Hurlbut 1969MS).
8. Background information on the 1874 excavation taken from Farquharson 1875; Gass 1877, 1877a; and Putnam 1886.
9. Farquharson 1875, 1876.
10. For discussion of Gass's trading of fraudulent relics, see Berlin 1886, 1886a, and chapter 8.
11. Farquharson 1875.

12. Chapter 11.
13. Farquharson 1876.
14. Gass 1877:81–82, 1877a:92–98.
15. Harrison 1880.
16. 1874 excavations pieced together from Gass 1877a and Farquharson 1875.
17. Farquharson 1875. Havana Hopewell is a recent identification.
18. Shetrone 1930MSa.
19. Although Griffin (1965:160) suggests the frog pipe may be a fraud, Shetrone (1930MSa) and McKusick consider it genuine.
20. Illustrated in West 1934.
21. Gass 1877a.
22. Gass 1877a:96.
23. McKusick's observations are based upon specimens and early photographs.
24. Pratt 1880a:256–57.
25. Questions asked in Foreman 1877MSa and Thomas 1885, 1886.
26. Farquharson 1877, 1877a.
27. Farquharson 1877:103–16.

CHAPTER 3

1. Baird correspondence of 1877 cited in Putnam 1886:342–43.
2. Foreman 1877MS, 1877MSa.
3. Advance copy published in Gass 1877a.
4. Foreman 1877MS.
5. Ibid.
6. See Pratt 1880a:193–202 for "Reminiscences" of the Academy.
7. Foreman 1877MSa.
8. Baird 1877MS.
9. Farquharson 1877a:65–66; Peet 1892:72, 1903:44.
10. Seyffarth 1882:72–80.
11. Chapter 1; Willey and Sabloff 1980:15.
12. Campbell 1882, 1883.
13. Campbell 1882:151.
14. Rust 1882:584–85.
15. Fleming 1977:72.
16. Fell 1976:261–69.

CHAPTER 4

1. Davenport Academy *Proceedings* 1877, 2:82.
2. Gass 1877, 1877a.
3. Putnam 1886a:119-20.
4. Harrison 1880:221–24; Tiffany 1882MS.
5. Hurlbut 1969MS.
6. Thomas 1885:564.
7. Harrison 1880:221–24.
8. Thomas 1885:564; Hurlbut 1969MS.
9. McKusick, personal observation of surviving specimens compared with original condition described in reports.
10. Putnam 1886:261.
11. Illustrating the uncertainty of acquisition, both Barber (1882:276) and Bailey

(1948:3–4) state that the elephant pipe was purchased for three or four dollars from the farmer Peter Mare; the curator, Pratt (1880c:349, note), and Farquharson (1880:67) both state the pipe cost five dollars. It was later alleged that Tiffany tried unsuccessfully to repurchase the pipe from Gass for his own collection and offered five dollars for it (see Pratt 1886MS and chapter 8).

12. Pratt 1880c; 349, note.
13. Blumer 1882.
14. See correspondence in Putnam 1886: 300–317 and chapter 5.
15. See chapter 13, especially table 13.1.
16. The numerous later tablet "discoveries" by Gass were quickly discarded from the Academy collections as obvious frauds and "plants," which discredited the limestone and slate tablets. There was almost no mention of them, although they represent prime evidence of antiquarian difficulties at the Academy. The Cleona tablets reported by Gass (1877c, 1880) were quickly disputed by Peet (1886:56) as too much of a good thing. A tablet from Sterling, Illinois, was also reported by Pratt (1882), but no illustrations survive that might show linkages with the slate and limestone examples that became so celebrated.

CHAPTER 5

1. Mason 1878:322.
2. Powell 1883.
3. Henshaw 1883.
4. Squire and Davis 1848; Uhle 1886.
5. Henshaw 1883:158.
6. Correspondence in Putnam 1886:300–317.
7. Harry E. Downer, *The History of Davenport and Scott County, Iowa*, vol. 1 (Chicago: Clark Publishing, 1910). It includes a chapter, "The Earliest Dwellers," pp. 31–44, that stoutly defends the authenticity of the academy relics.
8. Putnam 1885.
9. Putnam 1886:251–348.
10. Years ago, students in my introductory courses would sometimes pick up a copy of Putnam's vitriolic attack when visiting the Putnam Museum—and would "rediscover" the elephant pipes, asking me if I knew anything about the business. I was relieved when the museum's supply of the 1886 pamphlets finally ran out.
11. Selected quotations from Putnam 1886:300–317. Readers should consult Putnam to savor the full weight of the abuse heaped upon the scholars.
12. Uhle 1886 accepts the elephant pipes as antiquities.
13. Journal reviews from Putnam 1886:334–41. Again, the reader is directed to the compilation itself for the anger directed against the Bureau of Ethnology and its staff.
14. Putnam 1886 ibid.
15. Ibid., 341.

CHAPTER 6

1. Norris explored Hartley Terrace Oneota and Woodland sites with a horse-drawn rake and plow.
2. Tiffany 1876, 1876a, 1876b, 1876c, 1876d.

3. Tiffany 1882MS.
4. Thomas 1885.
5. Thomas 1886.
6. Ibid.
7. Ibid.
8. Putnam 1886a.
9. Ibid.
10. Ibid.
11. Thomas 1886a.
12. Ibid., 190.

CHAPTER 7

1. Peet 1879, 1880, 1884; cited in Putnam 1885, 1886.
2. Peet 1886.
3. Peet 1886:56.
4. Pratt 1882, circulated as a reprint before volume 3 was bound and issued. See also Gass 1877c, 1880.
5. Pratt 1886.
6. Ibid., 94.
7. Peet 1886a.
8. Putnam 1885, 1886:274.
9. Berlin 1886:99–100.
10. Ibid.
11. Thomas letter to Berlin in Berlin 1886MS.
12. Berlin 1886:101, includes the Stevens-Gass correspondence about relic trading and buying.
13. Stevens's letter published in Berlin 1886:101 and 1886a.
14. Putnam 1886MS.
15. Peet 1886MS.
16. Putnam 1886a replied to Thomas's charges; Putnam 1886b now used *Science* to defend Gass by forging a letter in order to defend the clergyman from the charges of fraud and relic selling made by Peet and Berlin in the *American Antiquarian*.
17. Translation of Gass's letter quoted in Putnam 1886b; this is the forgery referred to in note 16 above.
18. Putnam 1886b.
19. Putnam 1886b.
20. Gass 1886MS.
21. Personal observation.

CHAPTER 8

1. Tiffany 1882MS, quoted in Thomas 1885.
2. Thomas 1885, 1886, 1886a; Putnam 1886a, 1886b.
3. Putnam 1886a:119.
4. Tiffany 1882MS.
5. Tiffany 1886MS.
6. Thomas 1885MS.
7. Tiffany 1886MS.
8. Pratt 1886MS.

9. Smith's is the anglicized name of Schmidt's Quarry, located on the Cook Farm property and the source for the limestone found in Mound 11, according to Hurlbut 1969MS and chapter 14.
10. Harrison 1880, 1886MS.
11. Preston (1885–1886MS) kept the committee minutes during the Tiffany hearings and received documents from Tiffany 1886MS, Pratt 1886MS, and Harrison 1886MS; he wrote down Lindley's oral testimony, which was subsequently submitted to the Academy in writing as Lindley 1886MS.
12. Preston 1885–1886MS.
13. Ibid.
14. Lindley, recorded in McCowen 1886MS, minutes subsequent to the Preston minutes. The third set of minutes, the Lindley hearing, was recorded in Phelps 1886MS.
15. There is independent confirmation of both Tiffany's ownership of the quartz crystal before it was put in Mound 11 (Hurlbut 1969MS) and the grease-soaked elephant pipe forgeries (Shetrone 1930MS).

CHAPTER 9

1. Thomas 1886.
2. Following the Tiffany committee report (Preston 1885–1886MS), there was a general meeting to discuss it. This meeting was held 26 March 1886, and the minutes were taken by McCowen (1886MS).

CHAPTER 10

1. Phelps chaired the Lindley investigating committee, and these later minutes (Phelps 1886MS), the third of the series, are ascribed to him, as there is no mention of a recording secretary. Phelps 1886MS includes in the minutes all testimony by Lindley, the Grahams, and Pratt; supporting documents by Lindley and Pratt are listed separately in the References section.
2. Putnam in Phelps 1886MS.
3. Graham in Phelps 1886MS.
4. Lindley 1886MS.
5. Phelps 1886MS.
6. Ibid.
7. Pratt 1887–1889MS.
8. Phelps 1886MS.
9. Ibid.
10. Pratt 1887–1889MS.
11. Ibid.
12. Academy *Proceedings* 1893, 5:221–23.
13. Phelps 1886MS.
14. McCowen 1886MSa.
15. Ibid.

CHAPTER 11

1. Claypole 1886MS.
2. Anonymous 1886MS.

3. Jones 1886MS.
4. Peet 1886MS.
5. Peet 1891:266, 1892:76, 1903:47.
6. Wright 1886MS.
7. Latourette 1886MS.
8. Berlin 1886a.
9. Powell 1890:493.
10. Watson 1890.

CHAPTER 12

1. Harrison 1880.
2. *Rock Island Argus* 1887; Pratt 1887–1889MS.
3. Pratt 1887–1889MS.
4. Ibid.
5. Ibid.

CHAPTER 13

1. Thomas 1894.
2. Powell 1894:xli–xlii.
3. Thomas 1885, 1886, 1886a.
4. McKusick 1974:36–44.
5. Shetrone 1930MS, 1930MSa, 1930MSb.
6. During my examination, I made no chemical tests for grease. Linseed oil is said to have been used on some pipes.
7. Academy *Proceedings* 1886, 4:222–23; *Science* 1 (1883):205.
8. Shetrone 1930MSa.
9. McCowen 1886MSb.

CHAPTER 14

1. A photocopy of Bailey's 1947 report is now with the other documents in Special Collections at the University of Iowa.
2. The coroner ruled it suicide, but Bailey's friends suspected foul play, as he had no compelling reason to end his life. Hurlbut informally told me that suspicions centered on an English World War I veteran who was often around the museum and who acted strangely; it was argued that the hanging was *postmortem.*
3. Bailey 1948:3, 8–9.
4. Hurlbut 1969MS.
5. Huebinger and Associates produced a series of photographic albums and maps, but those at the State Historical Society in Iowa City do not include a photograph of the Old Slate House.
6. Hurlbut 1969MS.
7. Ibid.
8. Ibid.

CHAPTER 15

1. Basic information on Judge Bollinger is in the University of Iowa Special Collections, to which he gave his collection of Lincoln books and memorabilia. The dates and meeting places of the Academy are from the *Proceedings*.
2. Hurlbut 1969MSa.

CHAPTER 16

1. Gass 1886MS.
2. Putnam 1886b.
3. Gass, Erbe 1969MS.
4. Ibid.
5. Cited in Putnam 1886:264.
6. Gass 1882a.
7. Schroeder 1969MS. I rely on his typed notes, not having access to the newspapers in which these items about Gass appeared.
8. Ibid.
9. Ibid.
10. Ibid.
11. Ibid.

CHAPTER 18

1. Fell 1976, 1980, 1982.
2. Numerous examples listed in McKusick 1979a.
3. Fleming 1977:72.
4. Fell 1976:262–65.
5. Hunt 1975–76.
6. Fell 1976:270.
7. Thomas 1894. Grave Creek is identified as part of Ohio Adena culture, which preceded Hopewell; see Willey 1966:268–73. Silverberg 1968:103-4 discusses the Grave Creek fraud.
8. Fell 1976:158.
9. Cazeau and Scott 1979.
10. Fell 1976:160.
11. Ross and Reynolds 1978.
12. Goddard and Fitzhugh 1978.
13. Ibid.
14. Nicolaisen 1979.
15. Neudorfer 1979.
16. Hencken 1940.
17. Trento 1978.
18. McKusick 1979a.
19. This subject is a complex one, and the paranormal literature is a distinct problem for professional archaeological reply, since it is to a large degree separate from antiquarianism. I have published on aspects of these paranormal cases in *Nature, Journal of Field Archaeology,* and *Archaeology;* see McKusick 1982, 1984, and McKusick and Shinn 1980. These publications will lead the reader to this literature and to professional discussion by others.

20. Van Sertima 1976.
21. Epstein 1980 shows that all known coins are either fakes or not prehistoric.
22. Morison 1971:244–47; Godfrey 1955:40. An enormous antiquarian literature exists in support of faked runes and spurious Vikings.

REFERENCES

Publication abbreviations are *AA* for *American Antiquarian*, *AAAS* for *American Association for the Advancement of Science*, *Am. Nat.* for *American Naturalist*, *PDANS* for *Proceedings of the Davenport Academy of Natural Sciences*, and *USBE* for *U.S. Bureau of Ethnology*. Manuscripts are indicated by MS after the date; unless otherwise noted, originals are at the Putnam Museum, Davenport, with photocopies in Special Collections, University of Iowa Library, Iowa City.

Anonymous
    1886MS   Note to Putnam alleging collusion between S. D. Peet and Major J. W. Powell in rejecting the Davenport relics. Postmarked 22 January 1886, Washington, D.C. Signed "A Friend of Justice."

Bailey, John
    1948   An Unsolved Davenport Mystery. *Contemporary Club Papers* 52:1–19 (Davenport).

Baird, Spencer
    1877MS   Letter dated 26 June to J. Duncan Putnam, on Smithsonian National Museum letterhead, which rejects E. Foreman's report on the Davenport tablets.

Barber, Edwin A.
    1882   Mound Pipes. *Am. Nat.* 16:265–280.

Berlin, A. F.
    1886   Fraudulent Objects of Stone. *AA* 8:97–101. Correspondence.
    1886a   Fraudulent Stone Objects, and the Gass Correspondence. *AA* 8:228–30.
    1886MS   Letter to C. E. Putnam from Allentown, Pennsylvania, dated 9 January, quoting a letter Berlin has received from Cyrus

                          Thomas, Bureau of Ethnology, on the
                          fraudulent nature of the relics J. Gass
                          traded to H. C. Stevens.
1886MSa   Letter to C. E. Putnam from Allentown,
                          Pennsylvania, dated 28 January, quoting an
                          affidavit received from H. C. Stevens.
Blumer, Rev. A.
1882   Exploration of Mounds in Louisa County,
                          Iowa. *PDANS* 3:132–33.
Campbell, John
1882   Proposed Reading of the Davenport Tablets.
                          AA 4:145–53.
1883   The Mound Builders Identified. Abstract.
                          Proceedings of the AAAS 32:419–21.
Cazeau, C. J., and S. D. Scott.
1979   *Exploring the Unknown.* New York: Plenum
                          Press.
Claypole, E. W.
1886MS   Letter to W. H. Pratt from Akron, Ohio, da-
                          ted 6 February, discussing a geological
                          fraud at the Davenport Academy.
Epstein, J.
1980   Pre-Columbian Old World Coins in America.
                          Current Anthropology 21:1–20.
Farquharson, R. J.
1875   Recent Explorations of Mounds near Daven-
                          port, Iowa. *AAAS Transactions* 18:297–
                          315.
1876   Recent Archaeological Discoveries at
                          Davenport, Iowa, of Copper Axes, Cloth,
                          etc., Supposed to Have Come down to Us
                          from a Pre-Historic People, Called the
                          Mound-Builders. *PDANS* 1:117–43.
1877   On the Inscribed Tablets, found by Rev. J.
                          Gass in a Mound near Davenport, Iowa.
                          PDANS 2:103–16.
1877a   The Davenport Tablets. *Proceedings of the
                          American Antiquarian Society* 69:64–69.
1879   [Concerning Davenport Tablets] Corre-
                          spondence. *AA* 1:167–68.
1880   The Elephant Pipe. *AA* 2:67–69.

Fell, Barry
  1976   *America B.C.* New York: Quadrangle.
  1980   *Saga America.* New York: Quadrangle.
  1982   *Bronze Age America.* New York: Quadrangle.

Fleming, Thomas
  1977   Who Really Discovered America? *Reader's Digest,* Feb., 69–73.

Foreman, E.
  1877MS   Correspondence to J. Duncan Putnam from the National Museum, Smithsonian, dated 14 May and 22 June, in which Foreman rejects the authenticity of the Davenport tablets.

  1877MSa   "Report on Three Inscribed Slate Tablets from a Mound near Davenport, Iowa." Handwritten nine-page report on legal-size paper, headed in script "National Museum."

Gass, Erbe
  1969MS   Transcript of interview in Postville, Iowa, with Arthur Gass and Hertha Gass Erbe, son and daughter of the Reverend Jacob Gass. Recorded by J. N. Young, it concerns Gass's knowledge of the frauds. (Original, Davenport Museum.)

Gass, Jacob
  1877   [Note of a communication describing the stone tablets from Cook Farm Mound]. *PDANS* 2:81–82.

  1877a   A Connected Account of the Explorations of Mound 3, Cook's Farm Group. *PDANS* 2:92–98.

  1877b   Report of Exploration of Mound No. 10, Cook's Farm Group. *PDANS* 2:141–42.

  1877c   Description of Some Inscribed Stones Found in Cleona Township, Scott County, Iowa. *PDANS* 2:142.

  1878   Examination of a Large Mound in Jackson County, Iowa. *PDANS* 2:155.

  1880   Inscribed Rocks in Cleona Township. *PDANS* 2:172–73.

1880a   Report on a Mound in Jackson County.
                 PDANS 2:173.
1880b   Mound Explorations in Jackson County,
                 Iowa. *PDANS* 2:219-20.
1880c   Report of Exploration of Indian Graves.
                 PDANS 2:291-93.
1880d   Explorations of Six Indian Burial Grounds
                 in the Vicinity of the Mouth of the Rock
                 River. *PDANS* 2:354-55.
1882   Report of Exploration of Mounds in Rock
                 Island County, Ill., in 1879 and 1880.
                 PDANS 3:135-39.
1882a   Exploration of Mounds in Louisa County,
                 Iowa. *PDANS* 3:140-46.
1882b   Exploration of Mounds in Mercer County, Ill.
                 PDANS 3:147-48.
1882c   Ancient Fortification in Louisa County,
                 Iowa. *PDANS* 3:183-84.
1882d   Mound Exploration in 1881. *PDANS* 3:186-
                 93.
1886MS   Letter to W. H. Pratt, dated 13 April, Post-
                 ville, Iowa. German original not present.
                 This copy is an English translation and not
                 in Gass's handwriting, in which he admits
                 to being "the victim of all."
Gass, Jacob, and R. J. Farquharson
1880   Explorations of a Mound near Moline, Ill.
                 PDANS 2:289-90.
Goddard, I., and W. W. Fitzhugh
1978   Barry Fell Reexamined. *Biblical Archaeolo-
                 gist* 41:85-88.
Godfrey, William S.
1955   Vikings in America—Theory and Evidence.
                 American Anthropologist 57:35-43.
Gordon, Cyrus H.
1972   *Before Columbus.* New York: Crown.
Harrison, Charles E.
1880   Exploration of Mound No. 11, Cook's Farm
                 Group, and Discovery of an Inscribed Tablet
                 of Limestone. *PDANS* 2:221-24.
1886   Report of Mound Exploration near Pine
                 Creek, Muscatine County, Iowa. *PDANS*
                 4:197-98.

1886MS   Report to Fulton and the investigating committee relative to Tiffany's conduct, dated 2 January. Handwritten, two and one-half pages, legal-size paper.

Harrison, Charles E., and W. H. Pratt
1893   Additional Explorations at Toolesboro. *PDANS* 5:43–44.

Haven, Samuel F.
1856   Archaeology of the United States. . . . *Smithsonian Institution Contributions to Knowledge* 8, no. 2:1–168.

Hencken, Hugh O.
1940   What are Pattee's Caves? *Scientific American,* Nov., 258–59.

Henshaw, Henry W.
1883   Animal Carvings from Mounds of the Mississippi Valley. *Second Annual Report USBE:*117–66.

Hunt, Carol
1975–76   Correspondence on file at the Putnam Museum, Davenport, Iowa.

Hurlbut, Irving
1969MS   Judge James Bollinger's narrative, told to Hurlbut and John Bailey in the 1940s, concerning tablet and pipe frauds. Retold to McKusick and J. N. Young at Muscatine, 23 March. (Original, Special Collections, University of Iowa.)
1969MSa   Correspondence addressed to McKusick relative to the Bollinger narrative. (Originals, Special Collections, University of Iowa.)

Jones, William
1886MS   Letter to Putnam and Rogers, Attorneys, dated 12 April, Clinton, Wisconsin. It concerns a prospective libel suit against S. D. Peet.

Latourette, C. D., and D. C. Latourette
1886MS   Letter to C. E. Putnam from Oregon City, Oregon, dated 19 March, in which they agree to act in a libel suit against H. C. Stevens if there is a good case.

Lindley, Clarence
1876   Mound Explorations in 1875. *PDANS* 1:111–13.

1877   Mound Explorations in Jackson County,
                Iowa. *PDANS* 2:83-84.
1886MS   Statement that Lindley had personally seen
                platform pipes made in the Academy build-
                ing during the period from 1 January 1880
                through 1 January 1885. Sworn and nota-
                rized by L. M. Fisher, Notary Public, Scott
                County, Iowa.

Lynch, E. P., H. C. Fulton, C. E. Harrison, and C. H. Preston
1893   Mound Explorations at Toolesboro, Louisa
                County, Iowa. *PDANS* 5:37-44.

Mason, Otis T.
1878   Anthropological News. *Am. Nat.* 12:322-
                23.
1878a   "The Davenport Tablet" in General Notes,
                Anthropology. *Am. Nat.* 12:400.
1880   "Mound Builders" in General Notes, An-
                thropology. *Am. Nat.* 14:216-17.
1880a   "Another Elephant Pipe" in General Notes,
                Anthropology. *Am. Nat.* 14:455.
1880b   "The Davenport Academy" in General
                Notes, Anthropology. *Am. Nat.* 14:814-15.
1884   [Review of Henshaw in] General Notes, An-
                thropology. *Am. Nat.* 18:953-54.
1886   "The Davenport Academy" in General
                Notes, Anthropology. *Am. Nat.* 20:671-73.
1886MS   Letter to C. E. Putnam dated 1 May, on Na-
                tional Museum letterhead, concerning his
                reluctance to becoming embroiled in the
                Davenport controversy.

McCowen, Jennie
1886MS   Minutes of the 26 March general meeting of
                the Academy concerned with the expulsion
                of A. S. Tiffany. Handwritten. In photocopy,
                it covers eleven pages of legal-size paper.
                Originally transcribed on both sides of two
                extremely long sheets.
1886MSa   Minutes of the 28 May general meeting of
                the Academy concerned with the expulsion
                of C. T. Lindley. Handwritten and typed ver-
                sions. Originally misdated 28 June, typed

copies updated. Apparently taken down by a professional secretary, since Lindley had protested inaccuracies in the earlier March minutes, this handwritten copy was corrected by McCowen and is sixteen pages in length. (There is a second version, typed without original, having many inaccuracies, which cannot be attributed to McCowen. It emphasizes Lindley's guilt in making fraudulent relics.)

1886MSb   Notes taken of Lindley's testimony at two meetings.

McKusick, Marshall

1970   *The Davenport Conspiracy.* Iowa City: University of Iowa.

1974   A Perspective of Iowa Prehistory 1841–1928. *Wisconsin Archaeologist* 56:16–54.

1979   The Davenport Conspiracy: A Hoax Unraveled. *Early Man* 1:9–12.

1979a   The North American Periphery of Antique Vermont. *Antiquity* 53:121–23.

1979b   Canaanites in America: A New Scripture in Stone? *Biblical Archaeologist* 42:137–40.

1979c   A Cryptogram in the Phoenician Inscription from Brazil. *Biblical Archaeology Review* 5, no. 4:50–54.

1980   Review of *Saga America*, by Barry Fell. *Antiquity* 54:354–55.

1980a   Prehistoric Vermont and the Antiquarian Revolt. *Vermont History* 28:183–87.

1981   Deciphering Ancient America. *Skeptical Inquirer* 5, no. 3:44–50.

1981a   Review of *Saga America*, by Barry Fell. *Archaeology* 34, no. 1:62–66.

1982   Psychic Archaeology: Theory, Method, and Mythology. *Journal of Field Archaeology* 9:101–18.

1984   Psychic Archaeology from Atlantis to Oz. *Archaeology* 37, no. 5:48–52.

1986   Deciphering Ancient America. In *Science Confronts the Paranormal*, ed. Kendrick

Fraizer. Buffalo: Prometheus Press.

McKusick, Marshall, and Eugene A. Shinn
    1980   Bahamian Atlantis Reconsidered. *Nature* 287:11–12.

Meltzer, David J., and William C. Sturtevant
    1983   The Holly Oak Shell Game: An Historic Archaeological Fraud. In *Essays in Honor of George Irving Quimby.* Anthropological Papers, no. 72. Ann Arbor: University of Michigan, Museum of Anthropology.

Morison, Samuel Eliot
    1971   *The European Discovery of America: the Northern Voyages A.D. 500–1600.* New York: Oxford.

Neudorfer, Giovanna
    1979   Vermont's Stone Chambers, Their Myth and Their History. *Vermont History* 47:79–147.

Nicolaisen, William
    1979   Celtic Place-Names in America B.C. *Vermont History* 47:148–60.

Peet, Stephen D.
    1879   Recent Mound Explorations. *AA* 1:109.
    1880   Report of Discovery of Elephant Pipe no. 2. *AA* 2:320.
    1884   Mound Explorations in Iowa. *AA* 6:276.
    1886   Are the Davenport Tablets Frauds? *AA* 8:46–56.
    1886a   The Points Involved. *AA* 8:117–19.
    1886b   "Pipes and Mounds" in Archaeological Notes. *AA* 8:256.
    1886c   Extra-Limital Animals and Mound Builder's Pipes. *AA* 8:308–13.
    1886MS   Letter to C. E. Putnam from Clinton, Wisconsin, dated 27 April, in which Peet bitterly complains about Putnam's threatened libel suit and general troublemaking. Peet states he will publish the Gass defense if it is actually written by Gass himself.
    1887   The Mastodon in America and the Mound Builders. *AA* 9:242–47.
    1887a   "Elephant Pipes." *AA* 9:250–51.
    1891   The Mysterious Race. *AA* 13:266–75.

| 1892 | The Mound-Builders and the Mastodon. *AA* 14:59–86. |
| 1903 | *The Mound Builders: their Works and Relics.* 2d ed. Chicago: American Antiquarian. |

Phelps, J. B.

1886MS   Minutes of the committee investigating the conduct of C. T. Lindley. It contains hearings and testimony, with reports and correspondence by Mr. and Mrs. Graham, Lindley, Preston, Pratt, Putnam, and Sheldon. The questioning by Lindley of the Grahams concerning pipe manufacture and Pratt's behavior, together with a full statement of Lindley's charges, makes this manuscript group a key part of the collection.

Pidgeon, William

1852   *Traditions of De-Coo-Dah, and Antiquarian Researches: Comprising Extensive Explorations, Surveys, and Excavations of the Wonderful and Mysterious Earthen Remains of the Mound-Builders in America.* . . . New York: Thayer.

Powell, Major J. W.

1883   Report of the Director. *Second Annual Report USBE:*xxx–xxxiii. (Henshaw's report.)

1890   Prehistoric Man in America. *The Forum* 8:489–503.

1894   Report of the Director. *Twelfth Annual Report USBE:* xxix–xlvii. (Thomas's report.)

Pratt, W. H.

1876   Report of Exploration of the Ancient Mounds of Albany, Whiteside County, Illinois. *PDANS* 1:99–104.

1876a   Report of Explorations of the Ancient Mounds at Toolesboro, Louisa County, Iowa. *PDANS* 1:106–11.

1877   Shell Money and Other Primitive Currencies. *PDANS* 2:38–46.

1880   On the Exploration of the Mounds on the Farm of Col. Wm. Allen. *PDANS* 2:148–50, 154.

1880a	Reminiscences of the Early History of the Academy. *PDANS* 2:193–202.
1880b	Curious Relic from the Cook Farm. *PDANS* 2:256–57.
1880c	Note on the Elephant Pipes. *PDANS* 2:348–49.
1882	Inscribed Rock at Sterling, Ill. *PDANS* 3:89–90.
1882a	Exploration of a Mound on the Allen Farm. *PDANS* 3:90–91.
1882b	The President's Annual Address. *PDANS* 3:151–57.
1886	The Davenport Tablets Genuine. *AA* 8:92–96.
1886MS	Report to H. C. Fulton, chairman of the special committee investigating the conduct of A. S. Tiffany. Pratt replies to various verbal and written statements made by Tiffany about the fraudulent nature of the tablets and elephant pipes, reporting the charges are without foundation. Dated January.
1886MSa	Report to the special committee investigating A. S. Tiffany. It concerns Tiffany's conflicts over Academy policy. Unsigned, undated, in Pratt's handwriting; probably dates from January 1886.
1887–1889MS	Notes to Putnam regarding the men on the opposition ticket, and a lengthy report on Lindley's activities during the period of his membership. He accuses Lindley of fraud in attempting to obtain compensation for his collection damaged in a state building. He also accuses Lindley of accepting specimens on behalf of the Academy and then putting them in his personal collection.

Preston, C. H.

1885–1886MS	Secretary of special committee investigating A. S. Tiffany. Minutes of the meetings from 30 December to 4 March, including the testimony of Dr. C. T. Lindley. Handwritten, five and one-half pages, legal-size paper.

| 1886 | Mound Exploration near Joslyn, Rock Island County, Illinois. *PDANS* 4:198-200. |

Putnam, Charles E.

1885	Elephant Pipes and Inscribed Tablets in the Museum of the Academy of Natural Sciences, Davenport. 1st edition.
1885MS	Copy of telegram to S. D. Peet, dated 19 December, accusing him of "miserable libel."
1886	Elephant Pipes and Inscribed Tablets in the Museum of the Academy of Natural Sciences, Davenport. *PDANS* 4:251-348. (Reprint of 1885 pamphlet with correspondence added.)
1886a	The Davenport Tablets. *Science* 7, no. 157:119-20.
1886b	The Davenport Tablets. *Science* 7, no. 171:437-39.
1886MS	Typed copy of letter to S. D. Peet, dated 20 April, in which he argues that Gass's defense must be routed through the Academy rather than being sent directly to Peet by Gass.
1887MS	Letter to W. H. Pratt, dated 31 January, requesting detailed information on the men who formed "an opposition" group to his leadership within the Academy.
1887MSa	Letter to the editor of the *Davenport Democrat* countering the published newspaper story in the *Rock Island Argus* about the factional fighting at the Academy. Eight typescript pages, the article is dated 5 February. (Note: a number of other manuscripts by Putnam are in the files but are not enumerated here.)

Reid, M. C.

| 1878 | Inscribed Stone of the Grave Creek Mound. *AA* 1:139-49. |

Rock Island Argus

| 1887 | Newspaper story, unsigned, headlined "The Factional Fight." It is subtitled "The Academy of Science at Davenport—The Elec- |

tion—Cause of the Trouble—All's Well That
Ends Well." Dated 27 January.

Ross, Anne, and Peter Reynolds
1978   Ancient Vermont. *Antiquity* 52:100-107.

Rust, H. N.
1882   The Davenport Tablets. Abstract. *Proceedings of the AAAS* 31:584-85.

Schroeder, Stan
1969MS   Excerpts from the newspaper, the *Postville Herald*, describing the career of Jacob Gass in the 1890s. (Original, Special Collections, University of Iowa.)

Schwartz, Douglas W.
1967   *Conceptions of Kentucky Prehistory.* Studies in Anthropology, no. 6. Lexington: University of Kentucky Press.

Seyffarth, G.
1882   The Indian Inscriptions of Davenport, Iowa. *PDANS* 3:72-80.

Shetrone, Henry C.
1930MS   Report to E. K. Putnam, "The Davenport Elephant Pipes and Inscribed Tablets."
1930MSa   "Memoranda on the Davenport Public Museum Pipes to be used in formulating a report."
1930MSb   Catalogue notes.

Silverberg, Robert
1968   *Mound Builders of Ancient America: The Archaeology of a Myth.* Greenwich, Connecticut: New York Graphic Society.

Snow, Dean
1980   *Archaeology of North America.* New York: Thames and Hudson.

Squire, E. G., and E. H. Davis
1848   Ancient Monuments of the Mississippi Valley: Comprising the Results of Extensive Original Surveys and Exploration. *Smithsonian Institution Contributions to Knowledge,* vol. 1.

Starr, Frederick
1897   Bibliography of Iowa Antiquities *and* Summary of the Archaeology of Iowa. *PDANS* 6:1-24, and 53-124. (Note: issued as sepa-

rate items dated 1892 and 1895, respectively.)

1897a   The Davenport Academy of Natural Sciences. *Popular Science Monthly* 51:83–98.

1897b   Circular of Suggestions Regarding Work in Archaeology. *PDANS* 6:340–43.

Thomas, Cyrus

1885   The Davenport Tablet. *Science* 6, no. 151:564.

1885MS   Correspondence with C. E. Putnam, dated 21 October, 3 and 17 November, and 5 December; handwritten. Thomas replies to the charges circulated by Putnam (1885) and denies that there is a government plot against the Academy. He outlines the evidence later published in *Science* in an attempt to warn Putnam that someone had planted the tablets and they are of recent manufacture. He gives Putnam long extracts from Tiffany's letter, but finally (5 December) refuses to send a facsimile to anyone but Tiffany himself. The heated Putnam replies are present in faded typescript copy. This correspondence establishes the fact that in the fall of 1885, the Smithsonian staff was acting professionally and properly in an effort to expose the frauds without harming the Academy or becoming involved in personalities.

1886   The Davenport Tablet. *Science* 7, no. 152:10–11.

1886a   The Davenport Tablets. *Science* 7, no. 157:189–90.

1894   Report on Mound Explorations of the Bureau of Ethnology. *Twelfth Annual Report USBE:*1–730.

Thompson, James

1892   President's Annual Address. *PDANS* 6:304–7.

Tiffany, A. S.

1876   Discovery of Human Remains in a Shell-bed on Rock Island. *PDANS* 1:42–43.

1876a   An Ancient Copper Implement Donated by
                     E. B. Baldwin. *PDANS* 1:59.
1876b   Pre-historic Cremation Furnace. *PDANS*
                     1:64–65.
1876c   Report on the Results of the Excursion to
                     Albany, Illinois, Nov. 7th and 8th, 1873.
                     PDANS 1:104–6.
1876d   Mound Explorations in 1875. *PDANS*
                     1:113–14.
1882MS   Letter to P. W. Norris, Bureau of Ethnology,
                     dated 27 October, in which he states the
                     limestone tablet is a fraud and implicates
                     C. E. Harrison. He further adds that the
                     elephant pipes were frauds and "planted"
                     on J. Gass.
1886MS   A statement prepared in his defense and
                     presented to the committee investigating
                     his conduct. Typescript, seven pages, legal-
                     size paper.

Trento, Salvatore Michael
1978   *The Search for Lost America: The Mys-
                     teries of Stone Ruins.* Chicago: Contem-
                     porary Books.

Uhle, Max
1886   Zwei prahistorische Elephantendarstel-
                     lungen aus Amerika. *Zeitschrift für Eth-
                     nologie* 18:322–28.

Van Sertima, Ivan
1976   *They Came Before Columbus.* New York:
                     Random House.

Watson, Warren
1890   Those Elephant Pipes Again. *The Natural-
                     ist* 4, no. 7 [Unpaginated publication].

Wauchope, Robert
1962   *Lost Tribes and Sunken Continents: Myth
                     and Method in the Study of American In-
                     dians.* Chicago: University of Chicago
                     Press.

Weiner, J. S.
1955   *The Piltdown Forgery.* Oxford: Oxford Uni-
                     versity Press.

West, George A.
   1934   Tobacco, Pipes and Smoking Customs of the American Indians. *Bulletin, Milwaukee Public Museum,* no. 17, pts. 1 and 2.

Willey, Gordon R.
   1966   *An Introduction to American Archaeology.* Vol. 1. Englewood Cliffs: Prentice Hall.

Willey, Gordon R., and J. A. Sabloff
   1980   *A History of American Archaeology.* San Francisco: W. H. Freeman.

Wilson, Daniel
   1876   *Prehistoric Man.* Vol. 2. 3d ed. London: MacMillan.

Wright, R. E., Sons
   1886MS   Letter dated 15 March to C. E. Putnam from R. E. Wright's Sons, Attorneys, Allentown, Pennsylvania, in relation to a possible libel suit against A. F. Berlin.

INDEX